THE CONTEMPLATIVE ☙ COUNSELOR

THE CONTEMPLATIVE ❧ COUNSELOR

A Way of Being

Rolf Nolasco Jr.

Fortress Press
MINNEAPOLIS

The Contemplative Counselor
A Way of Being

Scripture is taken from the *Holy Bible, New International Version*®, copyright © 1973, 1978, 1984 International Bible Society. Used by permission of Zondervan Publishing House. All rights reserved.

The "NIV" and "New International Version" trademarks are registered in the United States Patent and Trademark Office by International Bible Society. Use of either trademark requires the permission of International Bible Society.

Interior image: Andrei Rublev's "The Trinity" (Wikimedia Commons PD-Art).

Cover design and photograph: Kevin van der Leek Design, Inc.
Interior design: PerfecType, Nashville, TN

Library of Congress Cataloging-in-Publication Data

Nolasco, Rolf, 1967–
    The contemplative counselor : a way of being / Rolf Nolasco, Jr.
       p. cm.
    Includes bibliographical references (p. 131) and index.
    ISBN 978-0-8006-9662-7 (alk. paper)
    1. Counseling—Religious aspects—Christianity. 2. Contemplation—Psychology. 3. Pastoral counseling. I. Title.
    BR115.C69N66 2010
    253.5—dc22
                                    2010039750

The paper used in this publication meets the minimum requirements of American National Standard for Information Sciences—Permanence of Paper for Printed Library Materials, ANSI Z329.48-1984.

Manufactured in the U.S.A.

*For my mother, Lulu
and to the memory of my father, Rodolfo Sr.
who both started me on this
path of contemplation*

Contents

ACKNOWLEDGMENTS   ix

INTRODUCTION: CONTEMPLATION,
MINDFULNESS, AND COUNSELING   1

1. THE IDENTITY OF A CONTEMPLATIVE
   COUNSELOR   15

2. THE GIFT OF CONTEMPLATION AND
   MINDFULNESS   33

3. CHRISTIAN CONTEMPLATION:
   A WAY OF LIFE   53

4. CHRISTIAN CONTEMPLATION:
   A WAY OF BEING IN THERAPY   69

5. CHRISTIAN CONTEMPLATION:
   A WAY OF ACTION   95

6. CHRISTIAN CONTEMPLATION:
   A WAY OF WORSHIP   111

NOTES   125

BIBLIOGRAPHY   131

INDEX   135

Acknowledgments

This book, although written singularly by me, came out of a community of fellow sojourners who are on the path of contemplation. I would like to take this opportunity to express my deepest gratitude for their inspiring accompaniment.

First, I am particularly grateful to the Association of Theological Schools' Lilly Theological Research Grants for providing financial assistance during my sabbatical so that I could travel to various monasteries in the United States and Europe for research and writing. Along the way I have met several individuals, monks, and brothers and sisters in the Lord, who walked alongside me and gave encouragement, a place to rest, directions, and conversations that up to this day remain alive in my heart.

Second, my thanks go to all of my students at Providence Theological Seminary who showed enthusiasm and excitement about the project. They have been a great source of inspiration and challenge. Their commitment to the centrality of the cross in the work of counseling has emboldened my heart and strengthened my resolve to ensure that spirituality remains a focal point in my teaching, research, and clinical practice. Their prayers, curiosity about the progress of the work, and welcoming reception of the ideas presented in this book kept me focused and on track.

Third, I am also grateful to the Imbabazi Rwanda team, whose devotion to social justice made me all the more committed to training

Christian counselors to be active in both personal and social transformation.

Fourth, I would like to express my deepest gratitude to all of my clients, whose lives have become intertwined with mine and who have made me feel more human. I will be forever changed because of the journey we all took together.

Fifth, I would like to acknowledge the friendship of Evan Sorensen, Rob MacDonald, and Ed Novello, who have provided companionship throughout the writing process. Their wit and wisdom, comments on the manuscript, and playful approach to life made writing less isolating and lonely. I am also indebted to Susan Johnson of Fortress Press for believing in the project. Her confidence in my contribution to the subject matter is both humbling and a great source of motivation. I also want to express my thanks to my editor, Henry French, and his careful work with my manuscript.

Finally, to my family and friends, thank you for all the support and love that you have shown all my life. I will be forever grateful.

✌❧ CONTEMPLATION, MINDFULNESS, AND COUNSELING

A true sanctuary, even before the life to come,
is a heart free from distractive thoughts
and energized by the Spirit,
for all is done and said there spiritually.

St. Gregory of Sinai

Ours is a culture of mobility. And in the rat-race mentality it promotes, we often fail to live our lives fully. Somehow we have grown accustomed to being on auto-pilot, constantly moving and never stopping, always gunning for the next best thing, and forgetting to appreciate that we already have the most important thing—our life unfolding right here and right now at this moment. Driven by frenzied thoughts and a sensibility that favors action, performance, and results, we do not often have not enough space to even catch, let alone be mindful of one's breathing. And so we go about our lives almost mechanically with little or no awareness of the seed of contemplation buried deep within. This is as true of many, if not most, Christian counselors as it is of their clients.

We live by default, doing what we have been programmed to do. We have been conditioned to believe that busyness and multi-tasking are a mark of effectiveness, that human efforts and plans speed up positive change, and that vitality is acquired by activity. The cultural focus on *doing* as opposed to *being* that society privileges tends to

1

strengthen this conditioning. Unfortunately, Christian counselors are not exempt from this subtle and all too familiar conditioning.

Our understanding of the spiritual life often mirrors and affirms these values. We regard large, "successful" churches that are abuzz with programs and events with great esteem; we encounter and applaud lay parishioners and church leaders who are seeking after the latest "spiritual technologies"; and those of us who inhabit the walls of seminaries and other religious institutions often hear ourselves and our colleagues trumpet "success," "numbers," and "productivity" over faithfulness and a humble walk with God (Mi 6:8).

The child-like faith and solitude of the heart that we are called to live have been trampled by the illusory promises of self-sufficiency and self-assertion, cultural promises that all invade the therapeutic space.

Interior silence and the mindfulness it fosters are almost entirely unknown. The silence within is drowned out by a surround-sound society that proclaims "bigger is better, enough is never enough, and success (as culturally defined) trumps everything." Inevitably, the drive toward upward mobility results in a downward quality of life often marked by disillusionment, isolation, discontent, and mindless wandering.

Unfortunately, most individuals have grown accustomed to live in this manner, numbed, oblivious, and out of sync with the rhythms of their inmost self. However, there are also those who, through the dissonance of modern life, have come to hear the faint cry of their soul for quiet, rest, healing, mindful living, and communion with the God who made them and loves them.

We see glimpses of this yearning among people we journey with in counseling. In their hurried, noisy, often painful, often fragmented lives, they seek a refuge from the onslaught of competing demands, a momentary pause so that they can catch their breath, a safe space to rest their wearied souls, a freedom they have never known, and a silence and solitude where they might get to know themselves and God.

Impacted, if not assaulted, by an insecure and distracted society, many who seek out a Christian counselor cry out in anguish not just for relief from symptoms but for that healing that is experiential and integrative in nature. No longer will they settle for mere pious words in response to the deep ache in their soul, nor will they accept a temporary and quick fix for the existential problem of estrangement. Instead, they call for an approach to healing that addresses, in a holistic manner, their broken selves and fractured relationships and enhances their capacity to live meaningful and connected lives. Meeting the pressing needs of such individuals takes the form of a spiritual healing that includes and yet also goes beyond resources contained in psychology and religion. The contemplative approach to healing introduces them to a different experience of self and relationships along with new levels of meaning-making and wholeness.

Integral to this healing is an exploration of connecting points between the client's unique story and the transcendent Christian narrative in a manner that engages body, mind, and spirit. In other words, a different approach to Christian counseling is envisioned—a healing encounter where the experience of inner transformation discloses the client's true identity (Gen 1:26; Gal 2:20) and permeates all aspects of his or her being-in-the-world.

It appears that the appeal for a more holistic approach to counseling—one that engages body, mind, and spirit—has not gone unheeded. In the marketplace, we find stacks of books on spiritually-oriented psychotherapies[1] that fuse religious resources and diverse therapies in the service of those seeking care and counseling. Prayer, Scripture verses, meditation, even religious rituals are utilized more and more alongside various therapeutic techniques in support of the change initiative.

From the vantage point of Christian counselors, this should not be seen as groundbreaking at all. There always has been, in varying degrees, an amalgamation of religion, spirituality, and psychotherapy in the theory and practice of Christian counseling. What is rather unorthodox is to witness our secular counterparts, who in the past have considered anything spiritual as anathema to psychological well-being, adopting a bold and pro-active stance in incorporating quite explicitly religious and spiritual resources into their therapeutic work. It is as if Freud's negative appraisal of religion has weakened its grip, rendering secular psychology more hospitable and open to the role of religion and spirituality in human flourishing.

As a consequence, Christian counselors do not feel as excluded from their secular counterparts as they have in the past. Instead, they are becoming more deliberate and decisive in forging collaborations with therapists of different persuasions. Indeed, a common ground is being found, and diversity is coming to be seen as a resource instead of a roadblock.

The impetuses for these bridge building efforts are manifold and include: (1) the erosion of singularity in thinking and the promotion of multiple and connected perspectives and practices; (2) a heightened emphasis on treating the whole person as opposed to compartmentalizing the person's distinct yet complementary parts; and (3) the ongoing restorative efforts of God to heal a broken and fragmented world through various means and pathways. Christian practitioners and their secular counterparts are no longer driven by an unbridgeable spirit of competition or exclusion. As a result, they are now poised even more strategically to meet the complex needs of those hungering for a more comprehensive approach to healing.

In reality, the interface of psychology, theology, and spirituality in the practice of care and counseling is far more complex than merely blending psychological interventions with religious resources. Often, the manner in which these domains are brought together is significantly shaped by one's integration framework.[2]

For someone who prefers *technical eclecticism*, the use of dysfunctional thought record, for example, might be complemented with an exhortation to have the "mind of Christ" as a way to combat pathogenic beliefs surrounding the self. This integrative framework is focused more on choosing from an array of techniques deemed effective in eliciting change without subscribing fully to their theoretical underpinnings.

Another counselor might practice spiritually oriented cognitive-behavioral therapy, an instance of *theoretical integration*, as a way of providing a more extensive procedure for dealing with low self-esteem. In this framework, the counselor is well versed in both the biblical counseling model and the cognitive-behavioral approach to psychotherapy, then extracts their commonalities, and fuses them together to form a unified strategy.

In like manner, a counselor might adhere to an *assimilative integration*, which enables him or her to explore and employ divergent perspectives and practices while remaining grounded in a particular theoretical orientation. A counselor might draw primarily from cognitive-behavioral therapy and then incorporate other modalities, both religious and otherwise, to complement and enhance his or her therapeutic work with clients.

As one can see, the terrain in which theology, psychology, and spirituality converge and diverge is more like a maze with many possible entry points than a straightforward map with clear-cut directions. In this complex process, there seems to be a need for flexibility and hospitality toward those who offer different yet complementary views so that change in one's own framework, when appropriate and needed, can be pursued.

There have been times in my own journey when a traveler from a different spiritual and psychological path offered a cup of wisdom and the bread of encouragement that furthered my journey. The encounter felt unsettling at first, yet the experience of accompaniment paved the way for shared dialogue, exploration, and discovery. The stranger-turned-guide became a fellow sojourner. Through mutual support we discovered a new vista from which to appreciate the steps each of us had already taken, and we found ourselves emboldened with the courage to discover new territories.

With a new set of eyes to survey the terrain comes an acute awareness of the trends and challenges arising from the amalgamation of modern psychology with Christian theology and spiritual practices. For example, the shift from a deficit model to a strength-focused and positive psychology model is a step in the right direction. However, when Christian counselors incorporate these new technologies into their work with clients without first unpacking their philosophical underpinnings, they implicitly endorse a humanistic agenda that sees the self as the prime mover and source of strength, courage, and determination in the pursuit of change. Slowly and with great subtlety this "selfism"[3] sidles into the psyche of these unsuspecting counselors who may then end up utilizing religious resources to help encourage the quest toward self-assertion.

In an age where secular humanism is in full force, it is often easy to be lured into the false promise of self-sufficiency as an adequate antidote to the problem of estrangement. We are led to believe that if we learn to be more self-governing and self-reliant we will be happier, more fulfilled, content, and more successful. Instead of risking ourselves to be more authentic and alive in our relationships, we adopt a consumerist mentality that tries to fill our inner void with objects and distractions, but which only succeeds in leaving us alone and lonely, insecure, disconnected, and empty.

Hypnotized by the popularity of self-help mentality, we slowly turn away from or pay mere lip service to the spirituality of self-denial, obedience, and surrender—a spirituality that, as we shall see, is nourished by contemplative prayer and mindfulness practices.

Unfortunately, the culturally pervasive self-help mentality has found a home in Christian counseling, and we often find ourselves swayed by the strong current of the larger culture that drowns out or dilutes our deepest convictions. Consequently, instead of opening to the healing presence of the Creator, we end up bowing before the known god—Self.

This cultural message, of course, runs counter to an understanding of Christian faith and life that moves not toward self-promotion but toward self-emptying (Phil 2:5-7), surrender, intimacy, and ultimately union with God (1 John 4:16). By departing from that understanding, we may end up endorsing, along with the larger culture, a portrait of the self as a self-made crystal vase that demands constant psychological polishing rather than as a delicate cracked pot, created, treasured, and redeemed by God.

When we fail to assist clients to take responsibility for their actions out of fear that doing so threatens our relationship with them, we merely help them string leaves together to cover their shame, guilt, and nakedness, thereby stunting the development of their moral agency and moral accountability. Every time we affirm a client's quest for happiness by ignoring the disavowal of commitments they have made to others, whether marital, familial, or communal, we run the risk of furthering their self-seeking behavior without any regard for the needs of others. We run the risk of trading the deep and healing values of Christian faith and life for the shallow values of self-sufficiency and self-aggrandizement. We end up ushering our clients away from the narrow path of surrender, intimacy, and union with God into another wider path that breeds restlessness and dislocation from their true home. Of course, a counselor cannot guide his or her clients toward that narrow path if he or she has not first made it his or her own path. The daily rhythms of contemplation and mindfulness help the counselor do just that.

The culture of individualism, consumerism, and quick fixes continues to creep into the work of the counselor whenever performance and quick results are the primary motivations. Often we get so extremely busy and preoccupied by our compulsion to quickly remedy "problems" that in reality require an unhurried transformation not only of the head but of the heart, that we grasp for the next best treatment available or hold onto tried and tested modes of intervention. Yet at the end of our therapeutic work we somehow get the sense that something is amiss and unfinished, that somehow all these theories and techniques have fallen short of responding to the soul ache that comes from a deeper, more primal place. Might an attitude of simply *being with* in the moment, of being open, hospitable, and curious, create a sacred space where this soul ache is replaced with soul rest? Might a shift in focus away from what we should be *doing* to how we should *be* in those moments help nurture the stance of *being with* in counseling?

In my own clinical practice, and when conducting peer and student supervision, I have observed and experienced a sense of pressure coming from the unwavering expectation that the counselor must immediately fix or provide solutions to problems presented by clients in therapy. This sense of urgency to act, combined with the counselor's need to perform and produce results, may create a frenzied atmosphere filled with the false notion and expectation that self-assertion alone is enough to deal with the human predicament of estrangement, dislocation, and discontent. It is precisely the tendency to act, often prematurely, in the face of pressure to provide quick solutions that perpetuates this notion.

But it does not have to be this way. Our action (doing) when it is born out of contemplation (being) has the potential to create an experience in which both the counselor and the client are held together by an experience of *being with*. In this experience, the first response is an attitude of full attention to the present moment; it is a hospitable, non-reactive, non-judgmental, patient waiting, thereafter leading to appropriate responses to what is unfolding in the present moment.

Sara[4] showed up for her second session distraught and in tears. Instead of my usual penchant to inquire, I restrained myself and waited patiently and silently for her to tell me her story at her own pace and in her own unique way of expressing it. I sat there in silence but fully engaged, honoring her need and unspoken request just to be with her, providing accompaniment with my undivided presence, void of any words or gestures to intervene. There arose an experience of *being with* marked by full attention, expanding hospitality, and purposeful response. Having created a space for Sara to experience herself fully, without interruptions or ready-made interventions on my part, we were both freed from the tyranny of having to "fix" her, and instead felt freer to explore multiple options to care for her.

Being grounded in and mindful of the present moment is a testament to our dependence on the sufficiency of the presence of God in directing our paths. Such complete surrender of all that we are and all that we do renders us more open to the ways and works of God. To put it differently, remaining on the path of surrender, intimacy, communion, and union with God shapes our being and doing with those whom God has placed in our care. Chapter 1 seeks to clarify the complexity of this terrain and offers another perspective by which these challenges can be addressed.

Therapy has the potential to offer a space where the weary can lay their heads and find rest, nourishment, and healing. Salient to facilitating a reparative encounter or corrective emotional experience[5] is the attitude that we bring as providers of care, an attitude which is colored by our beliefs about human nature, human relationships, and the process of change. The counseling perspective proffered here re-visions the identity of counselors (and by extension those seeking care) as inherently contemplative. It sees the therapeutic relationship as a space where contemplation is nourished and where change and transformation of the soul grows out of mindful and welcoming reception of the gift of the present moment. The contemplative approach to care and counseling paints an alternative therapeutic landscape and offers a response to the challenges that beset us these days.

It is important at this juncture to define key terms that will help frame our ensuing discussion. The word *contemplation* is used to refer to the loving and experiential knowledge of God. Following Gregory the Great, it is both a gift of God and a fruit of ongoing reflection on and reception of the word of God. Simply, contemplation is resting in the assurance and experience of God's love that permeates all aspects of our being:

> In this resting and stillness the mind and heart are not actively seeking Him, but are beginning to experience, to taste, what they have been seeking. This places them in a state of tranquility and profound interior peace. This state is not the suspension of all action, but a mingling of a few simple acts to sustain one's attention to God with loving experience of God's presence.[6]

The life of contemplation is nourished in many ways, including various mindfulness practices characterized by ongoing attention and a hospitable, non-grasping, non-judging, compassionate stance toward the gift of the naked now[7] as it is experienced interiorly and relationally. By mindful awareness of our breathing, bodily sensations, emotional states, and thought patterns, we clear our interior space so that the gift of contemplation can be received. As Mary Jo Meadow indicates, the non-discursive aspect of the contemplative life generates self-knowledge that leads to a loving knowledge of God and is a "particularly potent and direct method of purification for the nakedness of spirit needed for a very deep experience of God."[8]

The contemplative approach to care and counseling requires a primary commitment by the counselor to cultivate this loving and experiential knowledge of God. Such knowledge of (and being known by) God intimately frames the identity and function of the Christian counselor. The contemplative counselor lives and works out of the deep well of mindfulness, which opens up the possibility of living fully awakened and receptive to the gift of the present moment as shared and experienced by the therapeutic dyad.

By entering into the deep silence where God is known in love, the Christian counselor (and the client) begins letting go of the tendency to rely heavily on his or her own strength to facilitate the healing process and so becomes more open to the Spirit of God who makes everything new and redeems all there is. From a contemplative stance, all knowledge, skills, and techniques retreat to the background. What takes center stage is the self-emptying of all good and godly intentions, along with an openness to the healing power of *being with* oneself, the other, and God, while allowing that dynamic to dictate the process and outcome of psychotherapy.

When we approach counseling from a contemplative stance, we become more available and accessible to our clients and our minds become open and attentive instead of being consumed by the need to perform and deliver results. Such a welcoming stance is nourished not by self-assertion but by the self-transcendence that comes out of the silence and solitude within which the heart gazes upon the face of God.

The open reception to what is unfolding in the here and now and the conscious recognition of our dependence on God prepare the way of the Lord whose presence we acknowledge by being fully present ourselves. Chapter 2 delves deeply into this new way of living, loving, and laboring.

Central to the life of contemplation is the experience of the integration of body (through mindful breathing and awareness of bodily sensations), mind (through awareness of thoughts and emotions), and spirit (through prayer, *lectio divina* or holy reading, and other spiritual practices). This integration requires cultivation and must be ongoing and woven into the fabric of the daily rhythms of life.

The intentional pursuit of a contemplative life is both natural—it is who we are—and supernatural—it is a gift from God. The creation narrative reveals that humans are fashioned in an intricately integrative manner; from the dust of the ground God formed man and breathed into his nostrils the breath of life, and he became a living being (Gen 2:6-7). The contemplative life is grounded in both God's creative work and God's intentions for us.

Though the seed of contemplation is buried beneath all the distractions, zealous actions, and restless movements of our lives, it remains hidden and yet waiting to burst forth. What is naturally or inherently human cannot be denied or completely silenced; this seed of contemplation compels us toward a deeper communion with ourselves, others, and God. The hunger for intimacy and union is not satisfied through episodic spiritual or psychological regimens, but through daily and simple contemplative and mindfulness practices.

Personally, my own journey toward the contemplative life started years ago through an encounter with the writings of Thomas Merton and Henri Nouwen. As my spiritual guides, they provided a map to this ancient path that was simple yet demanding in its call to surrender all.

This journey led me to an experience so powerful it felt like a second conversion. At a spiritual retreat in Atlanta, Georgia, I experienced profound communion with God, not through words or gestures but through silence and solitude. Since then, every single day has been an opportunity to renew my commitment to a contemplative life through the regular practice of contemplative prayer and other spiritual habits of the soul, and through mindful breathing and other mindfulness awareness practices.

Tending to our interior ground results in a re-ordering of life and priorities. Silence, stillness, and solitude of the heart become norms for engagement and obedience, surrender and self-transcendence, all of which are responses to God's invitation to intimacy, communion, and action. The life of contemplation and mindfulness is discussed in depth in chapter 3.

As said previously, the contemplative life is integrative in nature. The seed of contemplation that is planted deep within grows fuller and richer, impacting all of life, touching and weaving together the realms of the personal and professional. Suffice it to say at this point that, when the daily rhythms of contemplative and mindfulness practice are integrated into the life of the counselor, he or she develops a way of being in therapy that will likely be markedly different from the way he or she was in therapy before taking up these practices.

Faithful adherence to these rhythmic movements (1) facilitates both a posture of openness and a non-judging, non-grasping presence and hospitality; (2) strengthens the counselor's ability to notice and attend to the textured experience of the client; and (3) highlights the need to discern and clarify God's ongoing presence, guidance, and direction in the therapeutic work. In other words, the contemplative way of being informs and shapes a particular kind of presence and a different way of conducting therapy.

For the contemplative counselor, this means a daily and intentional "self-emptying" of all "self-descriptors" (theological commitments, psychological training, clinical experience, and social location), and mindful awareness of the gift of the present moment. Such self-emptying and mindful awareness open the interior and relational space needed if we are to tend to God's presence and direction in the sacred therapeutic space.

Since counseling is intersubjective in nature, both the counselor and client are changed as a result of this encounter. Though this book is essentially about the journey of the counselor toward contemplation, it also explores the impact of this way of being upon the lives of clients. The contemplative and mindful stance of the counselor provides an opportunity for the client to have the same attitude toward him or herself. As the counselor notices without judgment the shifts in the client's internal processes, the latter discovers that he or she also has the capacity to be welcoming and compassionate toward his or her own subjective experiences. In other words, what is experienced relationally is slowly internalized by the client, becoming his or her own. This may include adopting certain contemplative and mindfulness practices introduced in counseling that support the nourishment of this new way of being.

Chapter 4 examines with sustained focus the personal and interior life of the counselor and the fruit it generates when linked with the professional practices of counseling. We shall also examine the impact of the contemplative and mindful stance of the counselor on the client's self-understanding and self-experiencing.

The contemplative life does not begin or end in the therapeutic hour. It both precedes and follows, and thus encircles or embraces, the meeting of two individuals who are bound by the commitment to *be-with*. It extends beyond this into a life that is characterized by a commitment toward positive social values. The restful and worshipful practice of the contemplative life provides counselors with the strength and quiet confidence to accept God's call to "to do justice, and to love kindness, and to walk humbly with your God" (Mi 6:8) with integrity and conviction. This commitment is demonstrated in two ways—personally within the particularity of the counselor's social location and professionally in the clinical context. The personhood of the contemplative counselor includes responsible engagement in simple acts of justice and the promotion of peace in the form of social advocacy and political activism.

Professionally, the contemplative counselor addresses issues such as racism, sexism, and classism embedded in the experience of the suffering of clients. The complex issues that clients bring to counseling, though intensely personal, are intricately linked to or shaped by the current social and cultural ethos. This psycho-systemic view of reality deepens the counselor's commitment toward the transformation of both personal and social worlds. Chapter 5 unpacks this seamless movement of contemplation and social action as experienced personally by the counselor within his or her social matrix and professionally in his or her work with clients.

The embodied and shared experience of God in the therapeutic sacred space has the potential to re-orient the relationship between the counselor and the client. During the course of treatment, the therapeutic dyad becomes increasingly aware that they are icons to each other, beloved of God and recipients of divine love in equal measure. Together they recognize their common bond by virtue of who they are in Christ and, out of that shared identity, they fulfill their unique and clearly defined roles in both counseling and in their life's calling.

It is within the context of mindful relationships, and not in isolation and self-preoccupation, that true and authentic selves are discovered. The self-knowledge that springs from encountering another leads to a deepening and loving experiential knowledge of the Other. Such experiential knowledge of God gives rise to an attitude of worship, awe, and reverence.

The surrender and humility characteristic of worship, awe, and reverence arise only from a heart that is open, still, and quiet. In a therapeutic encounter grounded in deepening mindfulness and contemplation and infused with a sense of worship and awe, both counselor and client are drawn into the healing mystery of God. Chapter 6 offers a glimpse of what it is like to sustain a life of contemplation understood as a life of worship.

This little book is written for Christian counselors with varying degrees of clinical experience. First, it aims at targeting seasoned practitioners who desire to reinforce their identity as followers of Christ not through external moves but through a journey inward. This will be particularly helpful to those who, through the course of time and due to increasing demands by the profession, have come to feel lost or disoriented with the persons they are becoming. The book offers an alternative path to rediscovering the call that started them off on the journey to becoming wounded healers. It also invites these clinicians to consider going beyond their default (often Western-based) theoretical tool box and engage resources from other religious and healing traditions in a conversation around unconventional ways of being in therapy.

Second, the book is also meant for those who have just stepped onto the path of becoming a Christian counselor. It offers a guide to novice clinicians who desire to anchor their identity in Christ as they venture into their vocation that is practiced in a largely consumerist, restless, insecure, and unhappy world. By grounding themselves in a place of mindful interior rest, they gain the inner strength and quiet confidence to do their work.

Third, the book is conceived with graduate students in counseling in mind as well. In this formative stage of their professional development, they will confront multiple voices clamoring for their attention and allegiance. This book offers an alternative voice that will be familiar yet new at the same time, affirming their convictions and inviting them to expand their horizon.

And lastly, those who are simply curious about the personhood and practices of a contemplative counselor may benefit from this work. Such readers will find a deeply personal account of formation and transformation that will hopefully inspire them to consider cultivating the seed of contemplation buried in their own interior garden.

The quote by St. Gregory of Sinai at the beginning of this introduction describes well the essence of this book: to illuminate that ancient path that will lead those who are hurting to a place where they can begin to heal, rest, and regain strength in the sanctuary of God that is found in their inmost self and in their lives with others. I have become convinced that the fulfillment of the Christian counselor's calling is significantly dependent on the counselor's willingness to journey with clients toward contemplation and mindfulness. The communal experience of *being with* will sharpen their loving knowledge of God and facilitate a keen sense of mindful existence, hospitality, and compassion toward themselves and others. The approach taken here goes beyond theory and techniques and is deeply personal in that it traces the journey I have taken toward a life of contemplation.

Chapter 1

❧ THE IDENTITY OF A CONTEMPLATIVE COUNSELOR

Spiritual knowledge comes through prayer, deep stillness,
and complete detachment, while wisdom
comes through humble meditation on Holy Scripture and,
above all, through grace given by God.

St. Diadochos of Photiki

Erin, a forty-five-year-old single mother, walked into my office on a dreary Friday afternoon with her usual gait—her shoulders lifted up, her back slightly arched, and her walk at slow cadence. She sat on the couch, almost in a fetal position, desperately trying to convey through her body what her lips could hardly express. Depression had taken over her life, and counseling was her last attempt at reawakening herself from its immobilizing spell.

We sat together in silence for the next five minutes or so and neither of us felt compelled to fill that gap with words. Then I began to wonder. Was her pain so heavy and beyond words that it rendered us mute? Had we both been touched by an experience that was, for the moment, best left unprocessed, without any forced re-description or quick intervention? Or was the silence a testament to my own sense of helplessness in the face of the enormous suffering that plagued her?

After a short while, she looked at me and in agony uttered the words: "Help, I am drowning." Something was markedly different about the way she expressed herself this time, I thought. Unlike other pleas for respite, this strained request seemed to emerge not solely from a place of deep despondency and dependence but also from a place of anger and frustration. Surely, the emotional tone of her desperation and discomfort was palpable given her circumstance, and yet somehow it felt as though there was more. As I began to explore what her request meant for her, it became obvious that a gnawing sense of discontent was beginning to bubble up inside her.

Suddenly she blurted these words: "What else can I do to get me out of this dark pit that I have been in for so long?"

I stopped dead in my tracks and let her anguish fill the space between us. I did not attempt to validate, empathize, explore, or interpret. We were both silent. Deep inside me, though, I felt her desperation and hopelessness. Every part of me wanted so badly to unlock the chains of depression that had held her hostage for so long. But I restrained myself from the urge to rescue and resolved to remain present and connected with her in silence.

We lingered there for a moment and we gradually realized that her cry revealed a place she had not been before—a deeper, primal place, a place of soulful anguish at the very core of her being.

What happened next will be discussed later in this chapter. Now I would like to describe possible scenarios in which the counselor's identity, relational stance, and theoretical orientation play a significant role in shaping the process and outcome of counseling in cases like Erin's.

A counselor tutored in and practicing a cognitive behavioral approach (CBT) would focus largely on exploring and challenging both Erin's maladaptive and negative self-talk and those behaviors she has adopted that inflame her depressive symptoms. Alleviating her symptoms would include increasing her level of awareness of cognitive distortions that reinforce experiences of helplessness and hopelessness through either keeping a daily journal or filling out a dysfunctional thought record. During therapy, Erin and her counselor would then process these materials as a way of disrupting pathogenic beliefs and replacing them with more realistic, adaptive, and healthy thought patterns. They would also develop alternative coping strategies, such as physical exercise, increased social contact, and the expression of needs, desires, and feelings, and would pursue the use of religious resources, for example, prayer, Scripture meditation, and fellowship, that Erin may find helpful in easing her suffering.

The identity of a CBT counselor can be described primarily as a "task master" who heightens the client's level of motivation or commitment to change, disputes his or her irrational thinking, and ensures that behavioral and spiritual interventions are carried out in and outside of therapy. The collaborative and educative nature of the therapeutic relationship is utilized as leverage for the adoption of an agreed upon plan of treatment.

A clinician who is using solution-focused therapy (SFT) would try to identify and magnify Erin's hidden and innate capacity to construct solutions to her problems. Instead of focusing on the problem of depression, the counselor will help Erin single out instances in which she has conquered depression, for example, taking the initial yet important step of seeking help or times when she went for a walk or chatted with a friend. Looking for exceptions would direct her attention away from the problem itself to times when depression was not as intense or not a problem at all. The positive orientation toward individuals coupled with specific solution-based interventions (for instance, miracle questions, scaling questions) that this approach promotes is a way of enhancing her belief in her self as a change agent, reactivating internal resources that are buried underneath and painting a satisfying future that is both promising and achievable.

The identity of a SFT counselor can be characterized as a "coach" who recognizes and makes explicit to the client his or her agency in charting an alternative path to change. This involves joining with the client to retrace steps by which change has already been made and imagining a horizon that is both full of possibilities and within the client's immediate reach. Like most therapies, a good therapeutic relationship is key in empowering the client to be intentional, proactive, and acutely aware of self-generated resources for constructing solutions.

Based on the examples above, it is evident that what transpires in counseling depends on a constellation of things—the client's readiness for change, the nature of the therapeutic relationship, belief in the restorative power of counseling, and the counselor's personal attributes and psychotherapeutic knowledge and skills, among others. The combination of these common factors in psychotherapy, according to a recent outcome research, is the heart and soul of change.[1]

Erin's cry for help seems to indicate her readiness to overcome her longstanding struggle with depression. Despite its debilitating effect, she still manages to show up for counseling and, with a sense of urgency, convey her need to be taken out of this "dark pit," as she calls it.

Half of the battle has already been won when a client like Erin shows motivation to change. The other half pertains to the therapeutic relationship itself which, according to the above research, is correlated with change.[2] The client's perception and felt-sense experience of the counselor is critical in determining the outcome of therapeutic work. Erin's bold request and openness to participate in the treatment regimen, when met with the counselor's empathic attunement, reflective listening, and validation, will intensify trust, safety, and security in herself, in the process of change, and in the therapeutic relationship. Consequently, the attempt at building and strengthening an alliance with her facilitates an active follow-through of treatment strategies.

USE OF SELF IN COUNSELING

Our personhood, or use of self-as-facilitator-of-change, plays a vital role in all of this. Our attitudes toward our clients, the lens that we use to filter and make sense of information or stories gathered, the therapeutic technologies we adopt and the lingering thoughts, feelings, and reflections we have before and beyond the therapeutic hour are heavily dependent on our self-perception and professional identity. Interestingly, a well-defined identity is not that easy to construct, define, and embody.

The therapeutic culture is in flux, and with it comes an array of possible options available to those trying to define who they are and what they do in counseling. For the most part, the formation of the counselor's professional identity rests on his or her accumulated knowledge and experience in providing care and counseling over the years. In other words, there is a certain degree of personalization involved in the process of establishing an authentic professional identity, but the emphasis remains on the counselor's demonstrated skills and competencies in providing treatment to clients.[3]

In the various therapeutic scenarios suggested for Erin's treatment, the counselor's identity is tied closely to a particular theoretical approach utilized in a manner that will reflect his or her unique personality and level of psychotherapeutic skills and abilities.

The formation of the Christian counselor's professional identity has a different entry point and is not solely based on acquired therapeutic knowledge and practices. When asked about their motivation for pursuing a career in counseling, most, if not all, of my students traced it back to an experience of being called by God to this specific Christian vocation. According to them, discerning their call involved an experience of congruity between their inner life and outer life.[4] That is, their personality traits and temperaments, interests, and motivations seemed to complement the core attributes and skills related to the task of counseling. As such, the learning and practicing of basic counseling skills may be seamless and natural rather than forced and inauthentic.

Fundamentally, the religious character of their vocation is grounded not in the profession of counseling but in their Christian identity. Their identity as a Christ-follower is the ground of their personal and professional formation as a counselor. In that formation, the Christian counselor experiences "a dynamic of freedom and response in [his or her] relationship with God . . . [an experience of living] one's life to the fullest, being open to change, and experiencing God's presence and blessings in the place, time, and work that occupy life."[5] Simply, the Christian counselor experiences no dichotomy between his or her core identity as a Christian and the profession of counseling. The work of the hands emerges from the state of the heart, and together they form a compelling case for incarnating Christ in counseling.

In a culture that expects quick fixes, advertizes self-focused makeovers and self-assertion, and offers a buffet of treatment modalities, the formation of a solid identity as a Christian counselor is often a challenging endeavor. Additionally, the voice of the larger culture, which is biased toward forms of spirituality other than Christianity and the proliferation of models of psychotherapy that are heavy on humanistic values, can all too easily drown out the counselor's inner spiritual convictions.

Some Christian counselors become disheartened and cocoon back to what is safe and familiar, while others are so easily swayed or influenced by all the spiritual and therapeutic options that they end up losing their bearing as Christian practitioners. Yet there remain those who are deeply anchored in their spiritual calling but are also curious and open to exploring other forms of healing. For these counselors, the challenge lies in knowing how to navigate new pathways to healing without eroding their core identity as a follower of Christ. Integral to this process is affirming one's Christian identity as the motive power and norm for seeking collaborative work with other disciplines, spiritual traditions, and healing practices.

Gifted psychoanalyst Carl Goldberg echoes the importance of the examined life, which is an internal journey, in the formation of the counselor's identity:

> For many practitioners deeply committed to meaningful therapeutic work, psychotherapy is not a conscious and rational vocational choice. It may sound unscientific, but in many ways I believe that it is accurate to regard the choice of practicing psychotherapy as a spiritual calling. As a spiritual calling, it imposes certain concerns, problems and hazards in the course of the practitioner's pursuit of a commitment to a way of life that transcends his/her professional hours. The practice of psychotherapy has as a foundation and basic tenet the pursuit of the examined life.[6]

For Goldberg the spiritual dimension of the practice of psychotherapy rests on the practitioner's descent inward in search of self. In that internal journey, the counselor is afforded the opportunity to examine openly his or her beginnings and to enter courageously aspects of self that are wounded and broken. Examining and embracing the "endless series of developmental challenges and frequent crises"[7] leads the counselor both to a deepened understanding of the nature of the human condition and to greater compassion and empathy for those who "petition us with their suffering."[8]

The counselor as a wounded healer derives his or her capacity to hold the pain and suffering of another by confronting his or her own adversity. Here lies both a paradox, "those who cure may remain eternally ill or wounded themselves,"[9] and a realization, "that illness can be a passageway in which one's real powers can transcend a given state of affairs . . . that his/her power to heal comes from the transformation of vulnerability into sensitivity, vision and compassion."[10] The counselor's identity, at least from Goldberg's perspective, is formed by accepting the call to self-examination and then using this interior journey to accompany and "guide others in their requisite voyages."[11] For this very reason, therapy may be seen as a spiritual pilgrimage toward self-discovery and the counselor as a spiritual guide that provides the needed accompaniment.

Goldberg's approach anchors the counselor in the constantly evolving terrain of psychotherapy without sacrificing the counselor's core identity and authentic self. The descent inward heightens awareness of self as a wounded healer, open yet discerning, broken yet resilient, and unfazed by the demands and challenges of counseling. The examined life is the best gift any counselor can offer to those who have "lost heart for that journey"[12] of self-discovery. And yet Goldberg's timely admonition stops short on one important thing; he ends with nothing besides a self that has come through adversity and ordeal.

In contrast, the formation of the identity of the Christian counselor as a healer does not end with the realization of the resilient self. The journey continues and hopefully leads to the discovery of another reality, that is, the dual discovery that our true identity rests on who we are in Christ (2 Cor 5:17) and that healing comes through the grace of God (2 Cor 12:9-10).

The most promising attempt at redefining the identity of the Christian counselor is offered by Mark McMinn, who claims that the best Christians counselors "are not only those who are highly trained in counseling theory and technique and in theology but also personally trained to reflect Christian character inside and outside the counseling office."[13]

Echoing this view, Timothy Clinton and George Ohlschlager specify roles and tasks[14] (such as reflective listening, physical and psychological attending, and empathic attunement) that every counselor, Christian or not, must perform. They then commend a list of spiritual disciplines (such as prayer, Scripture meditation, and worship) that should "first be alive in the life of the counselor, who then is able to give that life to clients and parishioners seeking help."[15]

Either used implicitly or explicitly in therapy, these spiritual practices become the defining trait of the Christian counselor. Clinton and Ohlschlager further claim that the use of these spiritual practices in counseling is "consistent with a pro-active, strength-focused approach to human change," and they argue that the work of spiritual formation serves to "feed our new nature in Christ."[16] As the work of spiritual formation helps us to "grow up into life abundant . . . we simultaneously starve our old nature, refusing to give place to the worry, doubt, fear, confusion, anger, vengeance and vanity that too often seethe within our souls."[17] In other words, the identity of the Christian counselor is closely tied to the pursuit and regular practice of spiritual disciplines.

Putting the spotlight on the practitioner's devotional life as an identity-defining factor is a step in the right direction. After all, these spiritual disciplines can be a fountain of strength, wisdom, and clarity that we can draw from as we accompany our clients on their arduous journey toward healing. Hence the clarion call to return to the basic spiritual practices of the Christian life needs to be taken seriously. However, there is the potential for this pursuit of holiness to turn into a subtle form of Pharisaic spirituality where the outward expressions of the religious life take precedence over the cultivation of the interior life. When the underlying ethos of a *works mentality* and *performance-based identity* gradually seeps into the psyche of the Christian counselor, the result may be the rather disturbing image of a counselor enslaved both by human strivings and by cravings for mastery and control.

To guard oneself from this potential pitfall, it is important to remember that the pursuit of holiness is the fruit of an interior life lived in communion and union between the Lover and the beloved. The closer we move toward the heart of God the more we realize, and embrace, the profound truth that we are deeply loved just as we are.

God's love for us is so unconditional and immense that the experience of this love moves us to simple obedience. The English word *obedience* is derived from the Latin word *ob-audire,* which means to listen. Hence, our first response to this great love is to listen intently, to incline the ears of our heart that we may hear the still small voice of God. Transformed by the experience of this love, we pursue holiness for no other reason other than to radiate the source of this great love to others.

THE IDENTITY OF THE CONTEMPLATIVE COUNSELOR

The loving and experiential knowledge of God that contemplation brings about is foundational in forming the identity of the contemplative counselor. Since contemplation is both a gift from God and a fruit of the mindful cultivation of the spiritual life, it follows that our identity, first and foremost, is a graced identity based not on merit but on our status as God's beloved. It is this divine love from which we came that we return to and proceed from. "If we find our true self we find God, and if we find God, we find our most authentic self."[18]

Therefore, the starting point in the formation of a Christian counselor's identity is the recognition and acceptance of his or her being as one created and loved by God. Such identity formation continues and is strengthened when the counselor enters into a life of contemplation grounded in the mindful cultivation of the interior life. Take the contemplative practice of *lectio divina* or divine reading, for example. Predisposed to listen deeply and attentively, the contemplative counselor bathes him or herself with the word of God on a regular basis, receiving it fully, letting the words come alive, not through discursive analysis, but by being open and curious to whatever God chooses to communicate. In a very subtle yet powerful way, the contemplative reading of the word of God works to transform the inmost being of the counselor into the likeness of Christ, who is the fulfillment of the Scripture.[19]

Out of the rich soil of a deep, loving, experiential knowledge of God springs forth fruits that the contemplative counselor can share with those who hunger and thirst for both healing and a fully awakened life. The fruits of contemplation are not our own doing, yet through us the fruits of contemplation are made available to all who come to us for counsel. The contemplative counselor may well become an icon to the presence of God in the midst of pain and suffering.

Before I entered the contemplative path, there were times in my professional life when the demands and challenges of counseling brought me to a state of inner turmoil and helplessness. Often the pain that clients bear is onerous and the pressure to "take away its sting" is immobilizing. In such instances, I have found myself hunting for every known intervention, both religious and psychological, that promised relief not only from my clients' symptoms but also from my own dwindling sense of confidence.

The anxiety these situations evoked within me at such times was fueled by a willful desire for self-assertion and results. Consequently, my identity as a professional Christian counselor became more a matter of reactive performance than a quiet presence, discerning, decisive, and deliberate, that endures in the face of suffering.

The life of contemplation I now participate in generates a deep undistracted centeredness, enabling me to enter into the pain of others with undivided attention. This makes me more accessible and available to my clients and to the unfolding of the present moment. Instead of worrying about the types of questions to ask or interventions to offer, I ground myself in who I am as God's beloved being, a person called to provide accompaniment to those hurting, using the gifts and graces I have been given to do so.

This book endeavors to reframe the identity of the Christian practitioner as a contemplative counselor who, in a humble walk with God, both receives and is energized by divine love. The experience of loving communion with God is deepened by the cultivation of the interior life through the contemplative practices of silence and solitude of the heart (Ps 46:10). These practices predispose the counselor to experience ever more fully the loving presence of God. The practice of mindfulness, with its emphasis on being awake, alive, attentive, and available to receive the gift of the present moment in a non-judgmental, hospitable way, supports the experiential and loving attention to God, who is fully with us in the present moment.

Being mindful of the presence of God gives rise to an interior peace that transcends all knowledge and understanding and guards the heart and mind from worries and anxieties that often beset the counseling context. With the peace of God permeating my body, mind, and spirit, I need not assert or exert my presence anymore or be scared by the depth of pain that my client experiences or be overwhelmed by the need for action and results. Instead, tranquility and a calm demeanor give me the freedom and flexibility to respond, and not react, to the tasks and challenges of the therapeutic encounter. With my mind uncluttered and fully attentive and awake to the present moment, I am more able to listen deeply and discern with clarity how best to accompany my clients on their journey toward healing.

My use of therapeutic skills and knowledge in ways that are meaningful and beneficial to the client originates from this place of quiet confidence, equanimity, and careful, deliberate thought. There is no need to rush toward the end goal; no need to counteract the ambiguity that often plagues counseling with ready-made and premature answers. Instead, this peace that transcends all understanding keeps me open to what is actually unfolding in the present therapeutic moment. I am at rest yet fully awake to the presence of God who hallows the space and is the true source of healing and transformation for those who suffer.

The experiential and loving knowledge of God and of oneself as God's beloved defines the identity of the contemplative counselor and renders the therapeutic process inherently spiritual and theological. The counselor's presence mediates God's presence in the face of human suffering. When we incarnate in our lives and labor God's comfort, peace, and healing, the therapeutic exchange evolves into a spiritual encounter with the living God, who is present in the here and now. This is to say that clients are no longer alone in their suffering In the presence of a contemplative and mindful counselor, the cry of their heart is heard, their suffering witnessed, and the isolation they experience supplanted by an experience of communion with another and the Other. Together, client and counselor (in the presence of God) set out on a journey, not by running away or hiding from pain, but by courageously accepting it as a guest bearing gifts of perseverance, character, and hope (Rom 5:4-5).

THE COMMON GROUND

I have traversed territories that, at first glance, might look foreign to each other yet, when seen through the eyes of contemplation, reveal a common ground that, when cultivated and nourished, yield fruit of many kinds. The rich traditions of Christian theology and spirituality, the field of counseling, Buddhist psychology and numerous encounters with clients, supervisors, colleagues, and students have all contributed significantly to my own evolution as a contemplative counselor. Traversing these various territories and going deep into their collective wisdom demands the practice of magnanimity.

> I think the metaphor of a world that grows simultaneously larger and smaller is what happens when we enter into dialogue with persons different from ourselves. On one hand, as the world expands, our hearts are challenged to grow larger, all-inclusive, universal—what mystics call magnanimity—living with a great soul and an expansive heart. . . . This wonderful gift, called magnanimity, usually catches us off guard when we venture into the unknown territory and allow our defenses to relax a bit. It is then that the other—the one who is different—shows us how much we really are one.[20]

One experience stands out as particularly formative in my learning both the art of encountering other traditions and the art of dialogue with those traditions. On my way to a spiritual retreat, I brought with me as my companions the writings of a Trappist monk, a Buddhist psychoanalyst, and the Bible. I can still remember how distinct their voices were, yet somehow together they formed a beautiful harmony, one that helped shape who I am today.

In Thomas Merton, the Trappist monk, I heard the simple melody of silence and solitude. In Mark Epstein, the Buddhist psychoanalyst, I discovered the importance of sustained attention to the unfolding of the present moment in counseling. And my reading of the Scriptures has been enriched immensely by an attitude of waiting in silence and acknowledging the presence of God in the here and now. I believe that I have become a better follower of Christ because my heart has been cracked open to receive the nourishment that comes from the common ground between diverse traditions.

Of course, engaging in dialogue is never easy. It can lead to dissent and division, especially when competition instead of communion, and arrogance instead of humility and respect, rule the day. To avoid such divisiveness and futility, we must enter dialogue with an attitude of listening—deep and respectful listening. We must enter dialogue with the expectation, if not conviction, that we have things to learn from others. According to Thich Nhat Hahn, the Vietnamese Zen Buddhist monk, this means that:

> In a true dialogue, both sides are willing to change. We have to appreciate that truth can be received from outside of—not only within—our own group. . . . We have to believe that by engaging in a dialogue with the other person, we have the possibility of making a change within ourselves, that we can become deeper. . . . Dialogue must be practiced on the basis on non-self. We have to allow what is good, beautiful, and meaningful in the other's traditions to transform us.[21]

Thich Nhat Hahn goes on to say that those engaged in dialogue with others must touch deeply the roots of their own tradition first before opening themselves up to the rich tradition of others. He hones this point by saying: "For dialogue to be fruitful we need to lie deeply on our own tradition and, at the same time, listen deeply to others. Through the practice of deep looking and deep listening, we become free, able to see the beauty and values in our own tradition and others' tradition."[22]

The practices of contemplation and mindfulness can assist in developing the capacity to fully inhabit one's own tradition while at the same time listening respectfully to and learning from the traditions and wisdom of others. The ongoing practice of *lectio divina*, for example, embeds the counselor deeper and deeper into the heart of God while transforming him or her more and more into the likeness of Christ. Anchored by the living word of God, the counselor then traverses unknown territory and hears multiple perspectives in therapy with an open heart—hospitable, curious, and respectful. In other words, listening deeply becomes a habit of the heart learned from daily contemplative prayer and mindfulness. The heart is primed to hear the heartbeat of another and together they discover that they pulsate as one, sharing the same human condition and promise.

The professional identity of the contemplative counselor is shaped by a deep and abiding experience and knowledge of God and the acceptance of one's standing as God's beloved. Use of the knowledge, skills, and practices related to counseling proceeds from that interior place where God is known in and as love. One form in which this love is expressed is genuine listening.

The approach I take is integrative in nature and the attitude that moves me is dialogical and exploratory. I bring together the rich resources of contemplative spirituality, counseling psychology and mindfulness to shed light on what it means to be a contemplative counselor. What I bring to this task is: (1) the awareness and acceptance of my own religious-theological location (evangelical); (2) a hospitable and curious stance toward multiple sources of wisdom and truth outside of my assumptive world (Buddhist psychology, mindfulness-based psychotherapies); (3) openness to living in tension, ambiguity, and unknowing; and (4) an acceptance and embrace of Mystery.

God's imprint is in all of creation, and as a person of faith, I take seriously the call to discern as best as I can God's continuing self-revelation and intentions for the world. Central to this undertaking is the willingness to transcend the familiar and encounter with discernment the unfamiliar, the yet to be known and the unknown. As the "Author of the Word and World,"[23] God accompanies me in the process of discovering truths from other traditions—psychological and otherwise—and expands my horizon so that I can see beyond my immediate subjective reality.

Though the path that I have taken is unique, I am not alone in this journey toward ever deepening intimacy and union with God. As a contemplative counselor, I am poised to listen to the testimonies of others, to appreciate the contributions of those who have gone before me, to see the validity and authenticity of various ways of knowing and experiencing God, and to use them as sources for self-criticism over and against the traditions that have shaped me thus far. In other words, contemplation generates both a sense of humility in sharing my discoveries and honesty in admitting my deficiencies.

The theological nature of this integrative task is primarily grounded in Jesus Christ, who is the "image of the invisible God" (Col 1:15). His incarnation provides a glimpse of what it is like to experience wholeness. He embraced with fullness and loving obedience both his humanity and divinity. His teachings, miracles, and relationships with people of various kinds reflect his penetrating transparency to God the Father as well as his steadfast commitment to bring all of creation back to the Creator.

The contemplative counselor gazes upon the face of God in Jesus Christ who, as an exemplar, reveals the power of reconciliation and asks us daily to pursue it in our lives. The division and fragmentation we all experience is the flipside of our deepest yearning for wholeness and union. The Lordship of Christ over all creation releases the potential in all of us to engage the unfamiliar, the unknown, and the different in a conversation that is dialogical, mutually rewarding, and ultimately God honoring.

The integrative nature that contemplation promotes requires a deep, abiding and personal relationship with the source of truth (Jn 14:6). Encountering the great I AM personally and intimately transforms our tendency to pay homage at the altar of self into a wholehearted devotion to the one God. It means offering everything that is descriptive of us to God who will transform and integrate our lives and relationships into a meaningful experience of wholeness and holiness.

A SNAPSHOT OF A CONTEMPLATIVE APPROACH

We now return to the case vignette presented earlier, only this time it is framed from the perspective of a contemplative counselor. Erin's cry for healing from the devitalizing impact of depression evokes a sense of urgency for intervention. However, as a counselor nourished by a life of contemplation, *the tendency to act is supplanted by a desire to be, to listen deeply, fully awake and attentive.* This means being available and present to the outpouring of Erin's anguish without probing, interpreting, reframing, facilitating a cathartic experience, processing residual or hidden emotions, or any other acts designed to contain this emotional cry for release. Instead, the counselor inhabits an interior peace and takes a posture of openness, curiosity, and hospitality to what is unfolding in the moment, without grasping or clinging to the urge to act or intervene, just letting things be as they are.

This models for Erin the possibility of her being available to her internal experience without the usual tendency to attach to (by rumination or getting overwhelmed by emotions) or to avoid (by psychic numbing) her thoughts and feelings. The theory of change that under-girds this process is that the contemplative and mindful presence the counselor exhibits releases Erin's capacity to become more aware and accepting, with compassion and non-judgment, of her own subjective and interior life. This creates the distance necessary for her to explore the myriad options available to her as she becomes more fully present and available to her own experience.

Developing Erin's innate capacity for meta-cognition being aware that she is aware of her conditions by simply noticing and observ-ing, enables her to de-identify herself from her thoughts, feelings, and reactions, which in turn increases her self-agency over her life. The counselor, from time to time, will coach Erin to describe or label her feelings as they arise, to try to locate them in her body and to enter both her body and the feeling fully by gently pressing against it with her hand. This emotional coaching heightens Erin's connection with the counselor, who bears witness to her pain and offers a quiet yet attentive accompaniment. By letting Erin symbolize what she feels in words, images, metaphors, or actions, she gains a different perspective of herself as someone who is able to regulate instead of being swayed helplessly by the sheer force of her experiences.

The counselor's contemplative and mindful stance is a clear indi-cation to the client that there is another way of relating to suffering, an attitude that is less adversarial and more welcoming. In a culture dominated by quick fixes and pain avoidance, this new way of deal-ing with suffering is counterintuitive. When suffering is embraced, however, we discover that we are resilient, that symptom alleviation is inadequate, that healing and transformation of character are avail-able to those who enter into it fully and compassionately. By listening attentively to the cry of her soul, she will soon discover her suffering is not to be carried alone, denied, or resisted, but accepted as one accepts a guest bearing a gift of renewal and connection. She will learn that in the midst of and beyond the ache is the faint, still, gentle voice of God calling her name and longing for her to come home.

The counselor's ability to stay engaged mindfully with Erin comes out of his or her ongoing commitment to live a contemplative life. The cultivation of the interior garden through contemplative prayer, silence, and solitude of the heart enhances attentional focus. Devotionally, it brings to mind both God's call for dependence and God's offer of accompaniment as the counselor and client descend inwardly into those places of pain.

When the counselor surrenders everything that is self-descriptive, including knowledge, skills, practices, doubts, lingering questions, and even good and godly intentions, for God's redemption and use, the therapeutic space becomes a place where afflictions are laid bare, acknowledged and accepted, and ultimately surrendered at the foot of the cross for healing and transformation.

The daily practice of mindful breathing affirms that our very breath is the gift of life from God. It is a concrete way of connecting the counselor to God, who sustains and enlivens the soul and whose love overflows beyond measure. Having been created by and for love, the counselor feels secure and grounded, lacking nothing and desiring only one thing—to be a channel of this diffusive love to others. And so he or she enters the therapeutic space with a clear sense of his or her identity in Christ, and is therefore capable of showing deep compassion and empathy for those who are hurting and have lost heart for the journey toward home. The contemplative counselor comes and offers peace in the midst of chaos, turmoil, and anguish, and in that quiet and still space suffering turns into dancing.

Chapter 2

&⧓ THE GIFT OF CONTEMPLATION AND MINDFULNESS

Attentiveness is the heart's stillness
unbroken by any thought.
In this stillness the heart
breathes and invokes,
endlessly and without ceasing
on Jesus Christ,
who is the Son of God and himself God.

St. Hesychios the Priest

In therapy, the counselor and client forge a special kind of relationship aimed at understanding and reducing the client's level of distress or suffering. Together they set out on a journey looking for a restorative path that soothes the ache of the human soul.

As they progress in their journey, they soon realize that there are many pathways to healing and that the trajectory itself may not be as straightforward as they would it like to be. There will be detours, rest stops, even winding roads along the way, but through the client's perseverance and faithful accompaniment by the counselor, both will eventually reach their destination. The journey's end, of course, is usually indicated by the client's experience of relief from suffering.

At the beginning of this journey toward healing, however, one often discovers a particular attitude toward suffering that is often implicit and tends to be negative, if not adversarial. In a culture that is saturated by numerous advertisements for painkillers and encourages the proliferation and easy access of mind-numbing substances such as alcohol and illegal drugs, lies a subtle message that says: *there is gain by avoiding pain.* The old adage "no pain no gain" seems to have lost its appeal and is now seen as a barrier standing in the way of pain-free success and social mobility. Since dealing with suffering demands time, attention, courage, and endurance, our culture supports denial of suffering through distractions and posturing. Though this psychological maneuvering may provide momentary relief, traces of anguish and ache linger on.

Sometimes therapy can be seen as a kind of painkiller. Clients come expecting to be relieved of their pain, and the counselor seeks to deliver that relief through various therapeutic means. With the emphasis on short-term intervention and increasing pressure from managed care plans, counselor and client are pushed to find the most effective cure in the quickest possible time. In this process, both counselor and client agree, albeit tacitly, on the notion that suffering is a foe to be conquered, a thorn that has to be extracted with great speed and urgency. In the end, what started out as an opportunity for inner transformation turns into a focused drive toward the alleviation of symptoms, which painkillers are strategically designed to do.

Might there be another way of relating to suffering that is less adversarial and reactive and more grounding and welcoming? What would the journey to healing look like if an attitude of compassionate acceptance and expansive presence pervade the counseling process?

Contemplation and mindfulness offer an alternative way of being in therapy and, by extension, a different way of seeing and relating to both the problem of human suffering and the experience of transformation. We have the gift of contemplation hidden within and therefore available to us right now in this very moment. This is referred to as *infused contemplation*, meaning that it is a direct action of God within us and not something that we can bring about through our own effort.[1] For the seed of contemplation to grow, however, it requires an active consent and participation from us. This is called *acquired contemplation* in which efforts are extended to align oneself to the will of God in our lives.[2] Through God's continuing outpouring of grace within us, and through various contemplative and mindfulness practices, there is an awakening of contemplation's quiet and yet life-changing work within us.

THE GIFT OF CONTEMPLATION

Contemplation is neither an approach to nor a technique in counseling. Fundamentally, contemplation is about a life in communion with God, an experienced union with the divine that yields the fruit of a transformed life that is fully awake and fully alive. It is both a *way of knowing* God and a *way of being* that mirrors Christ, who is the perfect image of the invisible God, in all of life.

As a way of knowing, contemplation is characterized by "self-forgetting attention, a humble receptiveness, a still and steady gazing, an intense concentration so that emotion, will and thought are all fused and lost [in God] who embraces them all. Gradually, by a deeper and deeper process of self-merging, a communion is established between the seer and what is seen, between him [sic] who feels and that which he feels."[3] Traditionally, this way of approaching God is understood as the culmination of a series of progressive devotional movements toward greater intimacy with God in which one proceeds from *spiritual reading* to *meditation* to *contemplation*.

As a form of prayer, *spiritual reading* uses passages in Scripture as the focal point for communicating with God. The chosen text is read slowly and silently several times until it sinks into the mind and heart of the pray-er. Bathed by the words of the living God, the pray-er develops a heightened awareness of, and consents humbly to, the loving and inviting presence of God in daily life.[4]

Spiritual reading provides a gentle nudge to the one who prays, encouraging him or her to go a bit further into *meditation*. In this second movement, listening to the word of God includes a reflection on how the words of Scripture can be made alive and real in the concrete and particular circumstance of the one meditating. This is often called discursive meditation because it involves reason rather than intuition, the use of words rather than interior silence; it involves memory and imagination, reasoning and feeling as a way of drawing out the implications of the word of God for daily life.[5]

Meditation leads to *contemplation*, in which where the first response is stillness and silence in the presence of a self-revealing God. As non-discursive, contemplation quiets all mental activities so the contemplative may be fully present and receptive to God, a receptivity "marked by naked faith, presence, and radical intimacy."[6]

Christian meditation can be classified further into two types, namely, attentional meditation and awareness meditation.[7] Attentional meditation chooses a single object—an image, an icon, a word, the breath—as the focal point of meditation. In Christian meditative practices, names ascribed to Jesus, such as light, the bread of life, the way, the truth, the life, are often used as an object of focus. These descriptors aim at deepening awareness of God's presence and transforming the meditator to be more Christ-like in character and disposition.

Unlike attentional meditation, which seeks to quiet the mind and draw the meditator into that interior silence where God is known in and as love, awareness meditation welcomes what happens or surfaces in the present moment in our thoughts, feelings, and bodily sensations, for instance, and listens deeply, but non-judgmentally to "whatever is being said," while encouraging the meditator to simply "be with whatever experience comes."[8]

An important form of attentional meditation in the Christian tradition today is Thomas Keating's centering prayer. A Trappist monk, Keating developed this meditative method to assist those who desire to deepen their relationship with God through silence. Centering prayer, a new name for an ancient practice, "is a method of silent prayer that prepares us to receive the gift of contemplative prayer, prayer in which we experience God's presence within us, closer than breathing, closer than thinking, closer than consciousness itself." This method of prayer is both "a relationship with God and a discipline to foster that relationship."[9] Based upon the anonymous fourteenth-century book, *The Cloud of Unknowing*, centering prayer uses concentration on the breath or repetition of a sacred word as a way of opening one's heart and mind to God, who is the subject of attention.

The spiritual focus of this practice is strikingly different from the current practice of mindfulness, where the emphasis is placed prominently on the individual. However, like its counterpart, when thoughts and feelings emerge during meditation, Christian practitioners are encouraged to simply acknowledge them, without grasping or analyzing, and to continue to lay bare one's heart, mind, and soul to God. The priority, according to Keating, is to be still, "like two friends sitting in silence, just being in each other's presence."[10]

The history behind the practice of centering prayer is rich yet singular in its accent on the experience of the immanence of God. The term used to describe this intimate encounter is *contemplation* or "loving attention," as St. John of the Cross described it, which starts with learning to "abide with attention in loving waiting upon God in the state of quiet."[11] The stillness comes from stripping the mind of all mental images, thoughts, emotions, and earthly concerns so as to focus on God Alone. Faith is integral to this process. The contemplative's intention and focused attention during contemplation is graced by the generosity of God who desires, "according to His free good pleasure, to communicate a glimpse of His majesty to the spirits of His servants."[12] All that is needed is to consent to God's invitation for communion in silence and solitude.

In the Eastern Christian tradition, this loving attention is expressed practically through the repetition of the Jesus Prayer or Prayer of the Heart in synchronization with one's breathing. The use of the prayer is the subject of a nineteenth-century religious classic, *The Way of a Pilgrim*, which narrates the story of a Russian pilgrim who desires to live out St. Paul's admonition to "pray unceasingly" (1 Thes 5:17). In his wanderings, he discovered a *staretz* (spiritual guide) who advised him to read the *Philokalia*, which contains sayings about prayer and spirituality from the Eastern Christian tradition. Yet of all the readings and conversations he had with the guide, one simple piece of advice stood out and unlocked the door of his prayerful heart.

> Sit down in silence. Lower your head, shut your eyes, breathe out gently, and imagine yourself looking into your own heart. Carry your mind, that is, your thoughts, from your head to your heart. As you breathe out, say, "Lord Jesus Christ, have mercy on me." Say it moving your lips gently or simply say it in your mind. Try to put all other thoughts aside. Be calm, be patient, and repeat the process very frequently.[13]

The pilgrim did exactly what he was told, uttering the prayer at first six thousand times a day and then twelve thousand times a day weeks later. The pilgrim soon realized that the Jesus Prayer had become as spontaneous and effortless as breathing itself. He had finally learned how to pray ceaselessly and through it experienced deep communion with God and all of God's creation.

The seemingly simple and formulaic pattern of the prayer is profoundly integrative at its core. Theologically, the prayer affirms the transcendent and immanent Triune God, who constantly draws people into an experience of true intimacy and abiding communion. The lordship and sovereignty of God in Christ are affirmed, not out of coercion but out of a deep recognition of one's cherished position in God's economy. As a created being, one's utterance of this prayer deepens awareness of one's dependence on God for everything; it is an invitation to pour out one's heart with reckless abandon and freedom. Practically, the Jesus Prayer brings together body (act of breathing), mind (bringing to consciousness the essence of the prayer), and spirit (the human spirit relating to God's Spirit) in one fluid movement.

As a way of being, contemplation quickens in us the desire to be transformed into the likeness of Jesus Christ, who is the perfect and complete image of the invisible God. His incarnation, death, and resurrection became the bridge to unity between God and humanity, and made it possible for us to dwell in communion with God. Hence, together with St. Paul, we are able to say, "And we, who with unveiled faces all reflect the Lord's glory, are being transformed into his likeness with ever-increasing glory, which comes from the Lord, who is the Spirit" (2 Cor 3:18).

Jesus unveiled our true self: made in the image and likeness of God (Gen 1:27). By simply gazing on the face of Christ we begin to see "who we truly are, who we always were, and this seeing helps us claim our deepest truth,"[14] that we truly are God's Beloved.

The contemplative vision of Christ's self-revelation produces a transformation within us that is so deep that we begin to discover the reality of our divine nature in each and every moment of our lives. Discovering this identity draws us closer and closer to the heart of God and there we realize "how wide and long and high and deep is the love of Christ" (Eph 3:18). To experience this "love that surpasses knowledge" is to "be filled to the measure of all the fullness of God" (19).

Imitating Christ in all aspects of our life is a clear expression of the presence of divine life within us. In fact, it is the only measure of true Christian spirituality. St. John of the Cross echoes this point by saying that "true progress lies in imitation of Christ, who is the Way, the Truth, and the Life . . . [Jn 14:6]. No spirituality is worthy of the name, which is based on sweetness and ease. Rather, we should imitate Christ."[15]

Following and imitating Christ is costly. It demands a willingness to follow the way of the cross, a willingness to embrace without any hesitation a "sharing in [Christ's] sufferings, becoming like him in his death" (Phil 3:10).

Once again, St. John declares that "those who take the spiritual seriously should be persuaded that the road leading to God does not require many considerations, methods, or unusual or extraordinary experiences . . . but one thing is necessary—self-denial and self-surrender to suffering and annihilation for Christ's sake. All virtue is contained in this."[16] The graced disavowal of our lust for self-assertion is an act of obedience to God who calls us to have the same attitude as Christ "who being in the very nature of God did not consider equality with God something to be grasped, but made himself nothing, taking the very nature of a servant, being made in human likeness" (Phil 2:6-7).

Through the spiritual practice of contemplation, gazing upon the lovely, serene, yet obedient face of Christ in stillness and adoration, we come to know who we truly are and what we truly are about. In short, the most authentic expression of the true self is a life in the Spirit that reflects Paul's confession: "It is no longer I who lives, but Christ who lives in me" (Gal 2:20). This graced existence peels off all superficialities and cravings of the exterior, insecure, and false self and unveils the "treasure in jars of clay" (2 Cor 4:7), the sweet and abiding presence of God within us.

Sadly, a multitude of individuals are out sync with or blind to their own divine nature. Instead of looking within to find their true identity, they put on a mask, a personage[17] that is crafted from a world that is lost and alienated from its true nature. With their faces turned away from God, and with the increasing cacophony of noise, activities, and cravings for self-possession and self-assertion inundating them, the still, small, and gentle voice of God who is calling them to communion is drowned out.

In spite of all this, however, there still remains within a faint yearning for something deeper and different—a way of being that is infused by an awareness of God's extraordinary presence in the ordinariness of daily life. Contemplation opens a door into this life of faith and authentic existence. When we dwell in the presence of God in stillness and with focused attention gaze upon the face of Christ, we see a reflection of our true nature as God's beloved children and realize that our vocation is a life of surrender, self-transcendence, and service.

THE GIFT OF MINDFULNESS

The experience of this sublime gift is available at every moment of our lives. Unfortunately, we are often so busy, so distracted, so self-absorbed that we fail to see the possibility of re-discovering and re-connecting with who we truly are. Mindfulness can heighten our ability to see beyond our exterior self and into the inner divine life that is always present.

Simply and yet profoundly, to be mindful is "to become completely alive and live deeply each moment of daily life. Mindfulness helps you to touch the wonders of life for self-nourishment and healing. It also helps you to embrace and transform your afflictions into joy and freedom."[18] It means approaching life with intentionality and hospitable attention to the richness and poverty, profundity and simplicity, pain and joy of our life as it blossoms right now, in this sacred moment.

The cultivation of mindfulness involves being aware of and attentive to the textured quality of human experience, the bodily sensations, states of mind, or the flow of thoughts and emotions as they surface in one's consciousness. The ability to be mindful of what is taking place inwardly in the present moment is supplemented by an attitude of non-judgment and acceptance, or letting things be as they are. Whatever arises or enters into the field of awareness, whether pleasant or unpleasant, is noticed not judged, welcomed not shunned, and labeled not analyzed. Such a non-reactive stance is vital in the experience of equanimity and stability.[19]

Mindlessness is the opposite of mindfulness, and in this state of mind one goes through life in an automatic and hurried fashion. One tends to be more impulsive, reactive and unaware of subtle shifts and movements in one's thinking and feeling. Such people often complain about their life being dull, lacking in depth and direction. In other words, they are merely existing, not living and thriving; however, when we live our lives deeply and mindfully, fully attentive to the gift of the present moment and what is unfolding in our lives right now, we put ourselves in the one place/time where divine healing can happen.

Neither contemplation nor mindfulness shies away from the reality of human suffering. Suffering is an inevitable part of the human condition, hence it is something to be expected and accepted, but with the confidence that it can be transformed, that true healing is possible. In the Christian tradition, the ultimate source of suffering is understood as alienation from God, and love is understood as the crucial starting point for dealing with human suffering. Contemplating God's ever expanding and sacrificial love compels us to face human suffering not with timidity but with great courage, confidence, and hope.

Thich Nhat Hahn, commenting on Buddhism's Four Noble Truths, says:

> The First Truth is the truth about suffering [*dukha*], and no one can see the path unless he or she sees suffering. . . . Everyone knows that if you run away from suffering, you have no chance to find out what path you should take in order to get out of suffering. So our practice is to embrace suffering and look deeply into its nature. . . . [By doing this] we find out what has created the suffering. If we have seen this, we know how to stop, to cut the source of nutrition for suffering, and then healing will take place.[20]

It is clear that in Buddhist philosophy the only way out of suffering is not around or away from it, but through it.

A GIFT TO THE CHRISTIAN COUNSELOR

Both contemplation and mindfulness offer the Christian counselor a markedly different way of dealing with suffering, and by extension, a different way of practicing counseling. Contemplation invites the counselor to prioritize above all else God's call for intimate union through the cultivation of the interior life. Focused gazing and loving attention on God highlights our utter dependence on God as the true and only healer and reconciler of disconnected selves and relationships. It also empowers us to embrace God's call for spiritual poverty, for emptying ourselves of all self-assertions so that we may be filled by the fullness of the Spirit (Gal 5:22-23). Hence, we embark on a journey with others in the dark valleys confident that God is our faithful companion who chose to follow the way of suffering in order to redeem it.

The experience of God's accompaniment during these moments of deepest pain, darkness, and vulnerability creates a sense of confidence and trust such that those who are hurting may be encouraged to embrace their suffering in the presence of another. In other words, it evokes a particular kind of presence, one that is stable, steady, and secure in our identity in God. As a result, we become both attentive and available to listen deeply to the anguish of our clients as we tend to their pain and suffering with compassion.

The development and growing popularity of mindfulness-based psychotherapies offer a glimpse of what this presence feels and looks like in counseling. What follows is a description of three mindfulness-based psychotherapies that consider attention and a non-judgmental attitude as central to therapeutic work with clients.

The Mindfulness-Based Stress Reduction (MBSR) program developed by Jon Kabat-Zinn at the University of Massachusetts Medical Center's Stress Reduction Clinic is a pioneer in this area. Supplementing traditional medicine, the focus of this program is on teaching patients with chronic physical conditions mindfulness techniques as a way of retracting themselves from automatic mental reactions that often impair their ability to handle stress well and solve problems. The MBSR is an eight-week program that teaches patients such techniques as sitting and walking meditation, guided body awareness, and yoga as a way of cultivating awareness of the unity of body, mind, and spirit. The focus is on ways in which our thoughts, feelings and behaviors influence our physical, emotional, and spiritual life. The ability to observe and notice while not identifying oneself with thoughts and feelings as they emerge in the present is pivotal in enhancing the quality of life of those suffering from intractable and chronic pain. Kabat-Zinn asserts:

> It is remarkable how liberating it feels to be able to see that your thoughts are just your thoughts and that they are not "you" or "reality". . . . The simple act of recognizing your thoughts as thoughts can free you from the distorted reality they often create and allow for more clear-sightedness and a greater sense of manageability in your life.[21]

Patients who went through the program reported positive physical outcomes, such as lowered blood pressure, and psychological outcomes, including reduction in emotional reactivity.[22]

Dialectical Behavior Therapy (DBT) is the brainchild of Marsha Linehan. It is an expanded form of cognitive-behavioral treatment combined with eastern mindfulness practices for multi-disordered (for example, depressed, anxious, substance dependant) individuals with borderline personality disorder (BPD).[23] A dialectical worldview, which emphasizes the synthesis or harmony of opposites, is the foundation of this approach to psychotherapy. The core dialectic in DBT is between *acceptance* of the client's current state or condition while concurrently recognizing the potential and ability he or she has to *change*. This radically replaces the rigid and dualistic thinking clients suffering from BPD tend to activate when confronted with threatening or stressful situations. Acceptance technologies in DBT include the core principles and techniques of mindfulness, such as attention to the present moment and taking a non-judgmental stance, for example, and other validation strategies. Change technologies are predominantly behavioral in nature, such as skills training, cognitive modification, problem solving techniques, and the like. Research has shown that clients who received DBT treatment evidenced "significantly less parasuicidal behavior, less anger, and better self-reported social adjustment."[24]

Mindfulness-Based Cognitive Therapy (MBCT), which took its inspiration from Jon Kabat-Zinn's MBSR, is designed to treat individuals who suffer from repeated bouts of depression. Developed by Zindel Segal, Mark Williams, and John Teasdale, MBCT brings together core principles of cognitive therapy and mindfulness practices and attitudes. Participants in MBCT are taught various mindfulness techniques such as mindful breathing, body scan, walking meditation, and others, to help them make "a radical shift in their relationship to the thoughts, feelings, and bodily sensations that contribute to depressive relapse."[25] Instead of automatic emotional reactivity or self-defeating ruminative thinking that gets activated when an individual is faced with stressful situations, participants take on the attitude of curiosity, openness and kindness, thereby giving them more options and possibilities to respond effectively. MBCT has been subjected to rigorous randomized clinical trials and the outcomes have been positive for those who have received the treatment.[26]

As shown above, the utility of mindfulness in psychotherapy as an alternative approach to promoting psychological well being centers on the cultivation of (1) awareness and attention (2) of subjective experience (3) moment by moment (4) with acceptance and non-judgment. Unlike traditional "talk therapies," these mindfulness-based psychotherapies hone in on teaching clients to become aware of what is unfolding in the present with no agenda other than to be with themselves with acceptance, curiosity, and openness. The non-grasping or non-identification with thoughts and feelings creates a wider expanse within, clarity and calmness, and fosters a more gracious attitude to oneself and, by extension, an experience of deep compassion and connection with others.

The application of mindfulness beyond the field of mental health is gaining ground even more. In another exciting and promising development, Daniel Siegel took mindfulness to another frontier by relating it to the life of the mind and advances in neuroscience. Awareness and attention, first and foremost, are mental events involving neural activities in the brain and, according to Siegel:

> When we focus our attention in specific ways, we are activating brain circuitry. This activation can strengthen the synaptic linkages in those areas. By exploring the notion that mindfulness, as a form of relationship with yourself, may involve not just attentional circuits, but also social circuitry, we can then explore new dimensions of the brain aspect of our mindful experience.[27]

Here, Siegel is making the bold claim that mindfulness has the capacity to harness neural plasticity, a term that refers to the amazing ability of the brain to change its structure and function, strengthening circuits that are used and weakening those that are rarely engaged.

A study conducted by Richard Davidson, of the University of Wisconsin, Madison, proved this point. The research compared the brain activity of novice meditators to that of Buddhist monks who had spent more than ten thousand hours in meditation. The participants were asked to practice compassion meditation, generating feelings of loving kindness to all human beings. The result was revealing. The brain scans of Buddhist monks compared to novice meditators showed a dramatic increase in brain activity during compassion meditation. With the aid of functional magnetic resonance imaging, scientists were able to isolate regions in the brain that were activated during meditation.

> Activity in the left prefrontal cortex (the seat of positive emotions such as happiness) swamped activity in the right prefrontal (site of negative emotions and anxiety), something never before seen from purely mental activity. A sprawling circuit that switches on at the sight of suffering also showed greater activity in the monks. So did regions responsible for planned movement, as if the monks' brains were itching to go to the aid of those in distress.[28]

The outcome of this study is quite exciting. Not only does mindfulness enhance internal attunement, it also leads to the activation of the mirror neuron system in the brain, which is the social circuitry responsible for inter-personal attunement via increased levels of empathy and compassion toward others.[29] The unifying effects of mindfulness strengthen the integration of body, mind, and spirit, which spills over from the personal to the social, from psychological being to pro-social and ethical values. The secure and fully alive individual who is internally attuned to the present moment with hospitality and openness is free to engage the external world with the "four immeasurables," specifically compassion, loving kindness, empathy joy, and equanimity.[30]

I have utilized a combination of these mindfulness-based therapies in my own clinical practice and discovered both their utility in helping clients deal with their painful experiences and their ability to disclose the workings of my mind. A case vignette might help elucidate the point that I am making here.

Judith came for counseling to cope with the loss of her marriage of sixteen years. She was well dressed, very articulate, and reflective in demeanor. She did not hesitate when I asked her what she wanted to accomplish in therapy. She wanted to deal with the lingering feelings of guilt for ending her marriage. Usually I would take this as a cue to explore sooner rather than later what those guilt feelings were, whether, for instance, she or her husband had done anything specific that prompted her to take this course of action. I would take it as a cue to look into the appropriateness of her emotional reaction and how she has been dealing with it. I would want quickly to explore if there was another feeling that was more pressing which she was unconsciously denying. I would want to know if there was a history of divorce in her family of origin and if her decision had caused her to feel shunned or questioned by family or by her religious tradition or faith communities.

In other words, normally my mind would be swirling with ideas on how to proceed to get a better understanding of who she is and the nature of her problem. But instead, this time I waited in silence and intentionally made myself available to her by staying fully present in the moment. I sat there with a focused and sustained attention to what was happening in her, within me, and between the two of us: her shortness of breath and pained look as if demanding a response; my own breathing that was deep and slow, and which rendered me both relaxed and expansive; the open space created by this momentary silence between us. Interestingly, as she watched me breathe deeply, she began to do the same and even made the comment that she had forgotten to notice her own breathing. I smiled and then we simply breathed in concert with each other. Below is a paraphrased account of what transpired at the beginning of the session.

Rolf: *Describe for me how you are feeling right now, and please do so without being critical about it.*
Judith: (She paused for a moment) *I feel guilty, anxious, sad, and ashamed.*

During this conversation I encouraged her to continue to breathe slowly and deeply from her diaphragm. I repeated her feeling-words back to her so that we could both hear them together again for the second time. This was my way of indirectly telling her that I heard her and that I was there to share her burdens with her. Toward the end of the session, I asked her:

R: *What was it like for you to simply observe and notice your feelings the moment they arose in your consciousness?*

J: *It was different because usually I would shut down emotionally and pretend that I don't feel them or ruminate about them and then get somewhat depressed or anxious or both.*

R: *So this is different because you are neither avoiding nor clinging to your feelings of guilt and instead, as per my instruction, you acknowledged the presence of these feelings, without judging them?*

J: *Yes.*

R: *How are you feeling now, knowing that there is another way of approaching your feelings?*

J: *I am not as afraid or confused or overwhelmed as I once was. Somehow, I feel ready to face them head on.*

Judith's last comment became my cue to go deeper, but slower, into her feelings of guilt, the details of which I will not go into here. I will describe instead the exchanges and the atmosphere that pervaded the rest of the session.

For the most part, we were able to sustain an atmosphere of tranquility and openness to what was taking place at the moment, for example, her tears falling down her face when she started talking about her two young children; the thoughts associated with her feelings of guilt; her fears and excitement around starting her life anew; and sadness for the loss of a very important relationship. We were both mindful of what was going on without any compulsion on my part to interpret or analyze or lay out a plan of action. We were both fully present, simply witnessing the ebb and flow of her multifarious experiences with an attitude of hospitality and acceptance.

The exchange was unhurried, soft in tone, restful, but fully awake and alert. I was very intentional in ensuring that I was fully present with her both internally in my mind and externally through my posture and mindful breathing. My mind was not racing or planning or scouting ahead for the next question or intervention nor was I thinking about the next session. It was at rest and attentive. My posture mirrored the same state of quiet wakefulness and openness. I planted myself comfortably on the chair, made few gestures or movements, and tried to be accessible and available as a witness to the unfolding of her experience.

The session ended, as to be expected, quietly. For an outside observer, the session may have seemed rather uninteresting, even disappointing, especially if they were looking for some specific intervention in response to the problem she presented. This is understandable given what we expect of therapy in general, namely a concrete solution given by the counselor to help lessen the distress of the client. From the perspective of a counselor who utilizes a mindfulness approach to treatment, however, fostering attention and a non-judgmental attitude to the client's unfolding experience in the present moment is essential in helping the client experience that expansive psychological and internal space necessary for subsequent work. This alone was significant for the client because it fostered within her an attitude of compassion toward herself and her subjective, fluid, and complex experiences.

Of course, counselors from a variety of theoretical persuasions can readily pick up on the techniques associated with mindfulness-based therapies. In reality, most counselors are already, in varying degrees, practicing the skills of attentive listening and non-judgmental acceptance of everything that transpires in therapy as it occurs in the here and now. For the Christian counselor who is inspired and shaped by the practice of contemplation, however, his or her presence is much more than a "therapeutic presence." It is ultimately an attempt to incarnate or embody the presence of God in the midst of suffering right there in that moment, with a willingness to be used by God as the earthen vessel of healing and transformation.

The impetus behind what I described above is deeply spiritual through and through. The attitude that a contemplative counselor brings to the task of counseling is suffused with an experiential and loving knowledge of God gained through the cultivation and regular practice of a life of interiority and assent. Such contemplative practice grounds the religious character of mindfulness awareness techniques in counseling.

Let me illustrate briefly the religious character of mindful breathing, attention to and living in the present moment, and the attitude of hospitality to emerging thoughts and emotions that are integral to mindfulness-based psychotherapies.

First, deep breathing has been proven to reduce stress, calm anxious nerves, and focus the mind. Sadly, the restorative and life giving quality of this practice has been largely ignored, especially in a culture that is so driven and obsessively active and restless. From a contemplative perspective, there is another dimension to breathing that includes yet transcends these positive outcomes. Drawing our attention with gratitude to the simple act of breathing is a way of remembering our deep connection with God who breathed into us the breath of life (Gen 2:7). We did not come into being on our own. Instead, we were mindfully and wonderfully (Ps 139:14) created by God whose image we bear (Gen 1:26-27). We are being held and sustained every day of our lives, and the air that comes in and out of our bodies is a concrete and experiential reminder of that reality. In the case vignette above, my own mindful breathing created an atmosphere of calm and tranquility both internally and relationally, which the client picked up on and stayed with as the session progressed. Mindful breathing was also my way of acknowledging that I am connected with God and that healing comes ultimately from him.

Second, the practice of living in the present moment is more than just a strategy aimed at enhancing equanimity and personal and interpersonal attunement. It is primarily a gift to be received and, when accepted, we discover that we are being sustained by the giver of life without whom we would cease to exist; we discover that our "being is suspended in God's presence."[31] This makes the present, as it unfolds moment by moment, sacred. Acknowledging the presence of God in this "naked now" brings clarity and vision on how best to live our lives with intention, depth and meaning. Firmly rooted in the ground of our being, we then approach life as we experience it in the here and now, with joy and gratitude because God is already here.

When working with Judith, I felt that I did not have to make things happen for her or guarantee results that she felt she needed or expected. I had already prepared myself for this encounter and had surrendered everything to God, including my skills and knowledge, intentions and desires, anxieties and questions, for God's blessing and anointment. This gave me the peace and assurance that we were both being held by God, which provided me both courage and hope in facing her suffering.

Third, the therapeutic benefits of simply noticing without judgment thoughts, feelings, and sensations as they arise in one's consciousness are many. As noted earlier, the practice of laying bare unpleasant experiences that originate from hidden spaces in our hearts disengages us from our usual reactive stance and widens options for change. By de-centering ourselves from the chatter of our minds, we discover that these cognitive and affective residues of our aching soul are transitory in nature. That is, they come and go when acknowledged, but cling like a magnet when we try to avoid or identify with them.

A contemplative counselor encourages the same non-anxious stance, but goes further than mere observation or acceptance of these painful experiences. Judith was encouraged to lay bare her suffering by noticing and naming it without judgment so that she could be fully acquainted with it. From there we explored, with an attitude of hospitality and curiosity, layers of unprocessed experiences in order to gain perspective and understanding.

Further along in our work together, however, we came to the point where she talked about unburdening all her pain to God, which became a significant therapeutic and transforming marker for both of us. We named all her pain and symbolically surrendered all of it at the foot of the cross, where ultimately the experience of courage, resilience, and transformational healing from our wounded soul can be found. Indeed, these painful thoughts and emotions, after they have been named and explored, do not just disappear to nowhere. They have a place and a person where they can be surrendered, and that place and that person is God (1 Pt 5:7).

Of course, not every therapeutic encounter leads to an explicit turning over of the client's cares and concerns to God. When this does not happen, it is important for the contemplative counselor to remember that God remains faithful and healing has already begun and is available to all, whether explicitly affirmed or not (Mt 5:45).

In summary, buried beneath our exterior self is a seed of contemplation waiting to grow and flourish. The seed of contemplation within us is a function of God's deep desire to be in communion with us. Our open and receptive response to this gentle and sweet invitation transforms our life in all ways. For the Christian contemplative counselor, this means a deliberate and sustained attention to the presence of God, one in which we are willing for the Spirit of God to transform us according to the likeness of Christ.

There are various contemplative and mindfulness practices that cultivate a life of interiority where God reigns supreme. Since the love and presence of God is diffusive, the counselor, through his or her life and labor, offers a presence grounded in the love of God that is compassionate, welcoming, and hospitable to the client and his or her suffering.

Chapter 3

❧ CHRISTIAN CONTEMPLATION: A WAY OF LIFE

"Watchfulness is . . . profoundly silent and still, and praying."

St. Hesychios the Priest

Roused by curiosity about the monastic life, I set off on a sabbatical journey that took me first to the cloistered walls of the Abbey of Gethsemane in Louisville, Kentucky, and then to Mt. St. Bernard Abbey in Leicester, England, and finally to the Taizé Community in France. At the entrance door to Gethsemane were the words of St. Benedict carved in wood: "Let all guests that come be received like Christ." I felt welcomed immediately and invited to experience the presence of God in their unique context.

This same gift of hospitality was evident throughout my journey, even from strangers on the street who gave me directions to these monasteries, who gave me a lift to the bus station, and who arranged for a place to lay my head during my travels. Though I was on my own, I was not alone for the Spirit was there to provide accompaniment.

Traversing the hollowed grounds of these monastic sites made me realize rather quickly the sheer force of silence, stillness, and solitude in opening up a world both strangely familiar and yet foreign at the same time. I felt lost and disoriented but, at the same time, eerily restful and at home. Indeed, behind these sacred and silent spaces lies a sweet and gentle invitation to rest in the presence of God, our true home. Soon the experience of being enveloped by the quiet, gentle, and still presence of God began to restrain my tendency to move around restlessly or preoccupy myself with work or earthly concerns. This led to an expansion of my own internal space so that I have more room for what God has to offer. Quickened by the spirit of God, I began to see clearly, through the monks' words and actions, that in these monastic communities "God Alone" is the rule of life.

The sight of monks streaming eagerly into the chapel for the liturgy of the hours seven times a day was a mirror to their focused commitment to contemplation. Everything stops and everyone returns to that nondescript yet womblike space where communion and union with God are so simply expressed in silence, in the chanting of the word of God, in prayer and meditation, and in the prostration of the body when singing the *Gloria Patri*. In other words, the rhythm of prayer, work, and study reaches its crescendo when the community marches silently yet eagerly into the chapel to gaze upon the Lord, the heartbeat of their life together.

Even more revealing and deeply humbling was to witness how these monks carried out their domestic duties. Whether they were receiving guests or vacuuming the rooms, preparing the meals or setting the table, their peaceful and joyful countenance was evident and infectious.

I had the privilege of spending some time with a monk at his pottery workshop, and there I understood what a labor of love truly means. His whole demeanor while molding the clay in his hands was a testament to an interior life that is enriched by a life of contemplation.

All of this pointed me to the transforming power of contemplation. Mary, the sister of Martha and Lazarus, chose it (Lk 10:42), the monks in those monasteries have made a lifelong commitment to it, and there I was, also invited, poised, and graced to make that same choice. An open mind and heart and mindful attention to the presence of God was all that God was asking of me. By the grace of God, the hurried and busy schedule I was so accustomed to was gradually replaced by a slower but intentional following of the rhythms of the monastic community. I worked when they worked and went to the monastery church when the bell rang to join the rest of the community in the liturgy of the hours. It was certainly a change of pace, a different way of being, and a more focused attention on God without interruption, which was something that had been missing in my life before entering those cloistered walls. My feeble attempt to consent to God's invitation to communion in silence and solitude, either alone or together, was met by an indescribable experience of God's expansive and enlivening love.

IN TRANSITION

Imagine how terrorized I was when I reintegrated back to the world I have always known. When I walked the busy streets of Louisville, London, and Paris, I felt disoriented, out of place and disturbed by what I saw. It was as if scales came off my eyes and I saw people differently. The swift pace of their steps, the sundry gadgets that adorned their bodies, and the dour look on their faces became strikingly more obvious to me, betraying something that I saw in myself as well. The never-ending chatter, hungry gestures for attention, and striking appearances were perhaps all just a front, a mask to cover selves that are insecure, lost yet longing for something deeper and different. The return to the world engendered both a feeling of nostalgia and a host of questions. Should I walk away from the world of complicity into the world of simplicity because I could no longer take the deafening noise that wreaks havoc within me? Is the impulse to recapture those special moments in the monastery more a form of escapism than a source of nourishment for my journey back into the world? Does a contemplative life have a place in a world driven by a mentality of quick fixes, surround-sound, and self-preoccupation?

I let myself linger with these questions and tried very hard to restrain the urge to offer perfunctory responses. It was not easy, however. I felt quite anxious not having answers to these pressing questions. What I am learning through this process is that at times questions do not always demand an immediate response. Questions need open and uncluttered space to settle, to come to rest like a butterfly on a flower so that, when ready to fly again, it will bring with it the seeds of answers. Poet Rainer Maria Rilke, indicated as much in his correspondence to a young man:

> I would like to beg you dear Sir, as well as I can, to have patience with everything unresolved in your heart and to try to love the questions

themselves as if they were locked rooms or books written in a very foreign language. Don't search for the answers, which could not be given to you now, because you would not be able to live them. And the point is to live everything. Live the questions now. Perhaps then, someday far in the future, you will gradually, without even noticing it, live your way into the answer.[1]

As a person and psychotherapist, I am uncomfortable living in tension or ambiguity, but I knew in my heart I had to learn how. With much struggle, tears, and perseverance, I discovered that loving the questions has gradually loosened my tight grip on the need for certainty and resolution and freed me to receive wisdom when I am ready. No longer imprisoned by my anxious mind, I began to pay more attention to what was before me, specifically going back to life, as I knew it. I felt as I returned to that life that I needed to do something different, something that would somehow mirror even slightly the rhythm of life I experienced in the monastery: beginning and ending the day in silence, chanting a few verses from the Psalms, and taking every opportunity during the day to silently pray the Jesus Prayer in concert with my breathing.

Life resumed and I found myself in the thick of things right away: teaching, counseling, reading and writing, chores, church, spending time with friends and family, watching television, or going to the movies. There were times when I skipped my morning or evening prayers or forgot to breathe prayerfully. Yet, deep inside me was this nagging sense that I needed to "slow down and breathe," which I did more consistently as I continued to follow this new rhythm of life.

The internal space that opened up during my monastic journey heightened my sensitivity to and desire for silence and solitude, especially when barraged with the noise, commitments, and chaotic pace of contemporary culture. I experienced the feeling of being pulled in two opposite directions. On the one hand, I felt myself being cajoled into a demanding external world that thrives on action, obligation, and the need to succeed. On the other, I felt an equally pressing invitation to retreat inwardly in silence.

Much to my surprise, it was this conflicted experience that led me to discover some of the answers to the questions I posed earlier. It was as if I had to live the questions first. It was not enough to raise the questions, I had to make a space for them in my heart, so that when answers came I was ready to receive them.

I discovered that being thrown back into a world without walls meant an ongoing uneasiness in the familiar accompanied by a deep yearning for something that seemed unreachable and yet so close. Choosing the path of contemplation has taught me to wait and to begin to let go of the intense need to understand or quickly find a resolution to my confusion. It has taught me to accept with kindness what is not yet known or what may remain unknown.

The discomfort I felt during these times of waiting and unknowing predisposed me to ask God for an extra measure of mercy and grace (Ps 27:14; 130:5-6). The lavish outpouring of divine consolation enables me to remain grounded and anchored in God while I continue to grapple with this tension. With the cloistered walls behind me and the challenges of life before me, I have learned to dwell in the abbey within, the interior of my heart.

The world around me has not and probably will not change anytime soon. I am still moving in and out of the classroom, teaching, advising, mentoring, and supervising. Therapy has become more involved in terms of the number of clients I see and the kinds of issues they bring. Relationships, whether familial, collegial, or social still require intentional care and presence. But something is qualitatively different in how I experience myself in all of this. The world continues to swirl around me, but somehow I still feel grounded in the present moment and aware that God is present in each moment.

Certainly these moments of clarity are not generated by my own willful attempt to be fully awake to the presence of the divine. Rather, they spring from a place within that has been profoundly awakened by the enlivening Spirit of God during my time at the monastery, and they continue to arise out of the stillness of my spirit as it gazes upon the face of God.

As silence grew within me, I realized the power it has in restraining my tendency to chatter my way up to the heavens. Stillness releases me from spiritual hyperactivity, and solitude prepares me to encounter God Alone. Because of this interior communion with God, I have begun to see people clearly and differently. I see that behind their cloak of appearances their inmost self is hidden with Christ in God (Ps 139:13; Jer 1:5; Col 3:3).

Yet the simplicity of silently turning inward is sometimes obstructed by the need for constant stimulation or connection with others. Even when alone and unoccupied, occasionally I find myself tied still to my computer or mobile phone as if they were a lifeline to the external world, without which I would be lost, cut off, or worse, feel like I had ceased to exist.

These old habits are difficult to relinquish, and yet in spite of them, the divine seduction continues. As Yahweh said of Israel: "I am going to seduce her and lead her into the desert and speak to her heart" (Hos 2:14). I have been seduced and led into the desert, and God speaks to my heart in the interior silence of contemplation.

Silence is not merely the absence of noise. In fact, a quiet room does not guarantee a quiet mind, though it helps foster silence. Conversely, it is also possible to experience silence amidst noisy and active surroundings. In other words, silence is more a matter of the heart—an attentive, watchful, vigilant, open, and receptive presence to God who resides deep within us. "God is closer to us than we are to ourselves,"[2] and with a gentle voice continues to call: "Come to me, my child." Yet the eyes of faith need to be awakened, and the ears of the heart need to be opened if we are to catch God's invitation to communion.

THE AWAKENING

Being illumined by the divine light through steady gazing upon God in silence has had a profound impact on my ways of living, loving, and laboring. As intimated earlier, my consent to God's invitation for communion in silence and solitude of the heart has created an expanding space within where my solitude may meet the solitude of others. The narrow and restricting nature of self-preoccupation has gradually given way to an attitude of hospitality where everyone is treated as guest. Being received as guest by complete strangers during my monastic journey has left an indelible mark and given me a real sense of belonging and wholehearted acceptance.

The self-giving attitude of the monks is shown in such simple acts as serving others first during meal times and, without being intrusive or overbearing, ensuring that all are seen, heard, and included during informal conversations. The monks seemed to have an expansive space within their hearts which allowed people to be free, to be who they are without restrictions or imposition. Integral to this self-giving attitude is the honoring of the distance between individuals that is essential to the flourishing of both individuals and relationships.

The number of people I come in contact with through my vocation as professor and psychotherapist is quite overwhelming at times, but my experience of hospitality has provided a different perspective on how these relationships are navigated. The expanding interior space that contemplation generates makes it possible now for me to receive each person in my life as an honored guest. I come as a host with no agenda other than to make room for them to breathe and find their grounding again. This then gives me ample opportunity to be anchored in the moment with them.

In my teaching, treating my students as honored guests helps me to allow them the time they need for the materials I am presenting to sink in. I don't try to hurry the learning process by bombarding students constantly with information. When I pose a question to the class, I usually encourage them to wait and let the question linger a bit in the air, so to speak, and so create a space within themselves to receive it. I have discovered that students are more engaged, even animated, when interacting with each other's questions in an unhurried, hospitable manner.

The same thing happens when I am involved in clinical work. Before I wasted no time in asking questions and launching into "talk therapy," now it is customary for me, after seating the client, to take a minute or so just to breathe deeply as a way of reminding myself, "I am here, present with you." I find this invigorating and focusing, especially when I see clients in succession. I have noticed that my mind, which is prone to discursive analysis, slows down when I take time to breathe prayerfully and I am more able to listen deeply and accurately. As a person who had been "talked out" in therapy once told me, "Clients more than anything else need a listening heart."

I have had my moments in therapy when I have been more active in speaking than listening, and in speaking without listening, but the gift of contemplation is changing that. Pausing for a moment lets the silence within me go deeper and wider so that I can receive clients not as patients to be cured but as sojourners to be accompanied. Their wearied and conflicted souls need a symbolic embrace from the therapist, one which says: "You are welcome here."

Clients are first and foremost persons with problems and not problematic persons; hence, as psychotherapist-host, my first gesture is to open the door of my heart and receive them like Christ would receive them. The accompaniment I provide, in whatever approach to psychotherapy we may take, springs from a place of interior silence, which brings about an attitude of hospitality.

There is another shift that happens when silence and hospitality take their rightful place in counseling. Eyes that have been opened through contemplation and mindfulness allow the counselor to see their clients and themselves as they truly are. While unique individuals, we are all reflections of each other; we are all human and, therefore, we all struggle with the problem of estrangement from the Divine. Estranged, but still created in the image of God, we are all potential bearers of divine light.

With my eyes open, I am now able to see past my client's symptoms or presenting problems into who they are in their essence. Though marred and broken by life, they are beloved of God and deserving of compassion, care, and focused attention. Listening, genuine and deep listening, is where this all begins.

Laurence, a forty-five-year old successful businessman, came to see me for counseling not long ago. He has struggled with depression most of his life and had been under the care of a few other therapists in town. He reported that neither medications nor psychotherapy had really made any difference, but he thought he would try counseling one more time.

Our initial consultation was spent doing paperwork along with intermittent personal anecdotes relating to his many losses, disappointments, successes, and dreams. I let him occupy our shared space with his stories, interjected a bit here and there just to get the facts straight, but mostly listened closely and intently. Toward the end of our first session, I asked, "Who have you become in light of all this?" There was silence. Then I said, "We don't have to answer this question right now, but I would like you to think about it."

He came back the next week, rather upbeat and excited, to tell me what he had discovered about himself when he reflected on the question. During our second session, he also mentioned something that brought immense joy into my heart and became the bedrock of the subsequent and painful work that we did together. He said simply, "You listened." This certainly did not cure his depression, but it was enough to let me accompany him in his journey to healing.

In counseling training, listening is a core skill that all students must learn. But there is another skill that I believe will complement genuine and deep listening. Students, as well as novice and trained counselors, need to learn the ways of looking deeply into the hearts of people. Like listening, this contemplative seeing illumines our true nature that connects us all together as one human family. Friar Vincent de Cousenongle, in his talks about "contemplation of the street," says:

> It does not mean walking around distracted in the midst of the crowd, but an attentive looking at all that surrounds us: these persons, these faces, their way of walking, the poverty of their dress. . . . [It is] knowing how to look for and understand what cannot be seen: failures, suffering, hopes. . . . It means to always make present now the human and divine gaze of Christ upon the crowd, the sick, all who are possessed by the evil of money, injustice, hatred. . . . This contemplation should be the privileged point of union in our lives between faith and the world.[3]

To summarize, awakening to the presence of God right here, at this moment, begins when we poise the ears of our hearts and the eyes of our faith to go deeper, beyond the external and into our inmost being. In this journey inward, silence is the rhythm that tunes us to the melody of God's love. Our consent to God's invitation to communion is both an expression and an affirmation of God's overflowing grace. Attending to our interior life, "without loud noise, no hungry movements, or impatient gestures . . . a place that want us to be silent, to sit or kneel, to listen attentively, and to rest with our whole being,"[4] is our way of subscribing in faith to the sufficiency of God Alone. Setting aside our insatiable desire to perform for an audience, to conform to the ways of the world, and to willfully take on the urge to reform is our way of receiving the grace of God that precedes, infuses and follows all human response.

I am not privileging a particular kind of spiritual discipline that we need to pursue to gain entrance into another domain of the spiritual life. No! Contemplation provides a path that will help us rediscover what I believe to be our primal and instinctual way of being in the world.

THE CALL TO CONTEMPLATION

A close, meditative, and repetitive reading of some of the texts from Scripture helps lay bare our innate hunger and thirst for God, who is the "bread of life" (Ex 16:16, Nm 11:11-14, Jn 6:35) and the "fountain of living water" (Jer 2:13, Jn 4:14). This became clear to me when I participated in the monastic liturgy of the hours, which consists of the psalms, hymns, and readings. Chanting the psalms gives voice to the deep longing of my heart for the presence of God. My experience resonates with Psalm 63:1-8, which declares:

> *O God, you are my God, earnestly I seek you;*
> *my soul thirsts for you,*
> *my body longs for you,*
> *as in a dry and weary land where there is no water.*
> *I have seen you in the sanctuary*
> *and beheld your power and your glory.*
> *Because your love is better than life,*
> *my lips will glorify you.*
> *I will praise you as long as I live,*
> *and in your name I will lift up my hands.*
> *My soul will be satisfied as with the richest of foods;*
> *with singing lips my mouth will praise you*

In the monastery, this entire psalm was chanted in an atmosphere of such great silence that every word carried profound meaning. They landed as drops of water in the parched desert of my heart and awakened within me the same desire expressed in the Psalm. The longing of my soul led to a profound gazing upon the face of God. There was nothing else that I could do or utter or offer except to lay before God a heart that was attentive, focused, and filled with awe.

A heart that becomes aware of its depth and the ground of its being is a heart that yields to a life that is doxological at its core. Contemplation, with its emphasis on silence and solitude of the heart, creates an opening for the body, mind, and spirit to be intertwined in seeking and singing the wonders of God.

God's desire that we live a contemplative life is reflected in Psalm 46:10: "Be still, and know that I am God; I will be exalted among the nations, I will be exalted in the earth." This verse ignited within me the divine impulse toward contemplation. I return to this simple yet profound invitation of the Lord time and time again, especially when I feel like I am straying away from the road less traveled.

Psalm 46 encourages the believer to hold onto God's abiding presence in the midst of uncertainly, instability, and fear. God's unquestionable loyalty and steadfast love ground the psalmist's call for a quiet confidence in God: "Be still and know that I am God." Despite the fear generated by nations warring against God and each other, by creation in chaos, with oceans roaring, mountains trembling, and kingdoms crumbling, God's call is to be still, to cease striving, to let things be.

One of the narratives that exemplifies a life of contemplation in a concrete and compelling manner is found in Luke 10:38-42. Johannes Vermeer's painting, "Christ in the House of Martha and Mary," captures in great detail the juxtaposition between two very distinct ways of attending to the presence of Christ. The visit of Jesus to the household of Lazarus, Martha, and Mary is met with expectation and enthusiasm. Martha, the ever reliable host, welcomed Jesus with her gift of hospitality, while Mary, the younger sister, expressed her thirst for his teaching and his presence by sitting at his feet. Both responses are very legitimate ways of receiving Jesus into their midst, but along the way, Martha got side tracked or felt overwhelmed by so much serving that she started complaining to Jesus about Mary's apparent unwillingness to help.

In his gentle rebuke, Jesus reminded Martha that ultimately "only one thing is needed and it is Mary who has chosen the better part"

(41). The two distinct yet complementary ways of receiving Jesus were differentiated quite starkly on the basis of Martha and Mary's attitudes and action. While Martha got busy, Mary settled in the presence of Jesus. While Martha offered her services to Jesus, Mary, unperturbed by the chaos and movements around her, received Jesus' offer of spiritual nourishment. The serene confidence in the sufficiency of Jesus Christ that Mary expressed so vividly "will not be taken away from her" (42).

During one of the evening prayers I attended in Taizé, we sang the German chant *Bleibet Hier*, which means, "Remain here with me, watch and pray." We sang this slowly and repeatedly, giving it a meditative character, and by the end of the chant, I experienced an abiding sense of being awakened into the presence of God. The chant is inspired by Jesus' experience in Gethsemane and his admonition to his followers to "watch and pray" (Mt 26:41).

The theme of wakefulness or keeping watch and praying can also be found in such passages as Matthew 24:42; 26:41; Romans 13:11; 1 Thessalonians 5:6; 2 Timothy 4:5; 1 Peter 4:7. In these passages, being awake and praying denotes being ready, fully attentive to the present moment, steady and steadfast in our commitment to and faith in the Lord. Such an awakened state is nurtured by silence and stillness within. These passages accentuate the value of closely attending to God's gentle presence in the midst of the chaos and noise of ordinary life.

These scriptural texts that commend the contemplative life can be summarized by the poet, Henry Wadsworth Longfellow:

> Let us, then, labor for an inward stillness—
> An inward stillness and an inward healing;
> That perfect silence where the lips and heart
> Are still, and we no longer entertain
> Our own imperfect thoughts and vain opinions,
> But God alone speaks in us, and we wait
> In singleness of heart, that we may know
> His will, and in the silence of our spirits,
> That we may do His will, and do that only![5]

STRANGERS TO THE CITY

Michael Cassey, a Cistercian monk of Tarrawarra Abbey in Australia, in his commentary on the Rule of St. Benedict, describes monks and nuns as "strangers to the city . . . [people who] consent to a different worldview, where previous priorities are turned upside down and a lifelong process of unlearning, learning, and relearning is initiated."[6] The cloistered life, communal rules and traditions, and personal commitment to live entirely for God help to foster this new identity. For those who are called to live a life of contemplation beyond the cloistered walls, however, the reversal of priorities and lifestyle, and the assumption of a new identity as contemplatives present different challenges and obstacles.

Recently, I had the opportunity to go back to Mt. St. Bernard for a time of silence, solitude, discernment, and writing. I left for London after spending some time at the abbey to see some friends and to prepare for my departure back to Canada. The train ride was just enough to give me time for reflection and preparation. As soon as I got off the train, a throng of people, mostly in a hurry, came rushing through the nearest exit. With my luggage in tow, I followed the swift cadence of Londoners, almost intuitively, as if we were being chased or chasing something or someone. After a few more hurried steps, I stopped all of a sudden, looked around and realized that I was no longer "a stranger to this city." I knew the drill and in an instant joined the frenzied crowd and felt like I had never left at all.

Upon reflection, I recognized that the transition from a world of silence to a world of surround-sound was marked by a sense of disorientation and disruption, a renewal of old patterns, and an awareness of the need to recover the new rhythms of life I have experienced through contemplation. In the words of Casey, the path of contemplation has introduced me to a "lifelong process of unlearning, learning, and relearning."

The transition has been painstakingly difficult, yet I was encouraged to attend to the piercing ache that filled me, not with judgment, denial or avoidance, but with curiosity, even hospitality. The "sharp-noticing-without-manipulation"[7] of my moment-to-moment experience in choosing between a life of contemplation (self-transcendence) and a life of distraction (self-assertion) has awakened me to the subtle and gentle stirring of the Holy Spirit and made possible the acceptance of my utter helplessness in the face of Mystery.

The instinctual pull toward the values and lifestyle of this age comes with such force that, without a disciplined but gentle movement deeper into the heart of God, we are left rather vulnerable. Our habitual ways of engaging the world—frantic, success-driven, and self-absorbed—are so ingrained and automatic that they can only be disrupted or un-learned by regular and disciplined contemplative and mindfulness practices woven together in daily life.

The contemplative life is a deeper way of knowing, one rooted in a "deeper ground of the heart that already communes with God, that knows only communion, as branches know deeply the vine."[8] The contemplative life renders the simple act of *breathing* into a way of deepening our connection with God who is the breath of life; it renders *hearing* into a profound listening to God's still, gentle, small voice; and *seeing* becomes a way of witnessing God in all things.

DESOLATION AND CONSOLATION

God's invitation to a life of contemplation is deeply personal yet it must be lived out within the context of community. During my early years as a contemplative, it was difficult to find individuals who could provide accompaniment on the journey. In fact, there have been moments when I felt all alone, isolated, and lonely. The pangs of desolation were often unbearable; they left me exhausted in all ways and disheartened at times.

Interestingly, there is something to be learned about experiencing the desolation alone and then seeking the company and comfort of others to help mitigate it. By allowing ourselves to enter the experience unaccompanied, we come face to face with the poverty of our spirit, which predisposes us to rely on and receive the abundant grace of God. As earthen vessels of God, we accept emptiness as an opportunity for the inflow of grace so that God is revealed in our weakness (2 Cor 12:9). In other words, the experience of desolation is essential to the contemplative's on-going call to self-emptiness.

The accompaniment that other sojourners provide is part of God's gift of presence during times of perceived absence. Yet, when seeking the comfort of others becomes our first response to the experience of desolation, it creates disordered attachments that often lead to feelings of rejection and dejection. We become too needy, too dependent, and even too demanding at times, and the comfort that we seek often turns into an insatiable need for reassurance and security. However, when we accept desolation as a guest bearing gifts, we are freed from grasping and possessing and develop an attitude of gratitude for its many surprises.

The contemplative life becomes the context within which the contemplative counselor approaches the practice of care and counseling. The pervasive experience of suffering associated with bare psychological wounds, spiritual hunger, restlessness, and the dis-ease of a "sin sick soul" is often met with pre-packaged remedies and pre-formed relational stances. Not so with a contemplative approach to counseling. The contemplative way of being in counseling sees the bearer of suffering as an honoured guest, the suffering itself a gift yet to be unwrapped, and the counselor a host whose primary agenda is to *be with*. The concrete outworking of this new way of being in counseling is the subject of the next chapter.

Chapter 4

CHRISTIAN CONTEMPLATION: A WAY OF BEING IN THERAPY

A heart that has been completely emptied of mental images
gives birth to divine, mysterious intellections
that sport within like fish and dolphins in a calm sea.
The sea is fanned by a soft wind,
the heart's depth of the Holy Spirit.
"And because you are sons, God has sent forth
the spirit of his Son into your hearts,
crying: 'Abba, Father.'" (Galatians 4:6)

St. Hesychios the Priest

The contemplative life is a way of fostering intimacy and communion with God, others, and self through on-going practices of mindfulness, silence, prayer, and solitude of the heart. These habits of the soul bring together, in harmony, disparate aspects of self, relationships, and tasks that have been compartmentalized or disjointed by a fragmented world. The cultivation of these practices in the interior garden of the soul sharpens our capacity to discern the movement of the Spirit of God and sustains our ability to become mindful of the presence of others through empathy and compassion. In other words, the unifying outcome of contemplation, first experienced in our interior and devotional life, spills over to our human relationships and engagements.

The flourishing of the connection between the interior and external worlds starts with an awareness and acceptance of the seed of contemplation that is planted within us, a seed just waiting to be cultivated and nurtured so that it can burst forth to life and bear fruit. The seamless movement of descending to one's interiority and then ascending to life with others is a rhythm that can be observed and practiced regularly in the unique context of counseling.

A contemplative and mindful approach to counseling proffers a distinct process of engaging clients with an attitude of *being with*. In this process, attention to the unfolding experience of the client and the relationship, moment by moment without judgment, permeates. It is essential to this way of being in therapy to lay bare both the basic predicament of alienation and the basic healing potential of contemplation and mindfulness.

Approaching the task of counseling in this manner is significant for a number of reasons. First, laying bare both the human predicament and human potential side by side promotes a more holistic, integrated, and realistic description of the human condition than any singular view would. The dialectical tension that arises from this paired view is closer to our felt experience as human beings compared to what is currently being promoted in the field. For example, too much emphasis on the pathology (deficit model) in clients may result in an excessively pessimistic stance, one which portrays the client as almost beyond redemption. On the other hand, too much emphasis on the client's inherent potential (strength model) may result in an excessively optimistic view of humanity, one which portrays the client as utterly self-sufficient. Such one dimensional portraits make us feel either less or more than what we truly are.

Second, promoting an attitude of hospitality and equanimity when the nature of the human condition is laid bare indicates a particular way of relating to suffering that is critical in the experience of transformation. It is through acceptance instead of aversion or attachment to suffering that healing comes about. Acceptance means looking deeply into our broken selves long enough to discover truths that will set us off on the journey toward healing. One of these truths is that symptoms are markers of an underlying condition that needs sustained and careful attention. When the core condition of estrangement is addressed, the attendant symptoms will likely disappear. This process involves accepting the reality that part of human nature is the capacity to heal. It also involves accepting that contemplation, as communion or *common-union,* is a way of promoting holistic healing and of mending both disconnection from oneself and estranged relationships with others. All this is hard to see if our first reaction to suffering is either to run away from it (aversion) or grasp onto it tightly (attachment).

Third, a contemplative approach to counseling emphasizes the relational aspects of both the problem and the pathway to healing. Estrangement is the breaking of union and contemplation is the healing of disconnection. Clients come for counseling because of disjointed relationships with themselves and others. The contemplative counselor, through increased empathy and compassion developed as a result of on-going and personal contemplative and mindfulness practices, offers an experience where the client can begin to cultivate intrapersonal integration and inter-personal communion.

The experience of transformation that a counselor attempts to facilitate involves being attentive and hospitable to the client's expressions of estrangement and disconnection as they surface in the moment. This means modelling for the client what it looks and feels like to gently notice, observe, and label internal responses or reactions—the thoughts, feelings, and sensations that the client is experiencing in the here-and-now—without grasping, evasion, or judgment. The mindful awareness, focused attention, and hospitable stance the counselor takes toward the subjective experience of the client and his or her suffering is the hallmark of this particular counseling framework.

As indicated previously, this is contrary to how most people deal with suffering, which can be described as either aversion or attachment defensive reactions. In fact, this response seems so conditioned that even the familiar story in Genesis 3 mirrors it. In the creation narrative, we witness the couple deal with the limits of their condition by attaching to and then acting out the illusory and false idea that they can be like God, knowing good and evil. As a way of avoiding responsibility for what they had done, they sewed leaves together to cover themselves and hid from the presence of God among the trees.

The response of God to their transgression is strikingly different from theirs. God searched for them and called them out of their hiding place so that they could begin to "lay bare" or acknowledge their action. But this was met with resistance. The couple grasped onto (attachment) their fear and shame of being naked and blamed each other, even God, for what had befallen them (avoidance). God, however, remained unperturbed by their refusal to accept their condition and situation, and provided a way of redemption. Called by God to participate in the work of redemption, the contemplative counselor embodies non-anxious presence, unconditional acceptance, and an unflinching belief in the power of faithful accompaniment in bringing about healing and transformation.

As indicated above, a contemplative vision of counseling presupposes certain views of human nature, the nature of the human condition, human suffering and the process of change or transformation. What is offered below is but a description of the essential elements of contemplative counseling and should not be taken as either definitive or exhaustive. It is presented as a map that hopefully will guide those who are interested in further exploring the contemplative terrain of the therapeutic landscape.

THE HUMAN CONDITION

The symbolic expulsion of Adam and Eve from the garden represents our own experience of estrangement from God. The chasm created by this relational divide has made us all exiles from our true home, estranged from our true identity, and severed from the source of true love. With the experience of estrangement comes a pervasive and nagging sense of dis-ease and dislocation that we desperately try to excise or deny. Banished from our true home we wander aimlessly, even unknowingly, searching for a place where we can rest or feel at home and experience deep and unconditional connection and affection. The dwellings we find and inhabit, much to our dismay, are transitional. These dwellings are not the home we long for and are a poor imitation of that eternal home in heaven for which we yearn. We yearn for that heavenly home where we can be in communion with God eternally.

Estranged from our true identity, we lack both authenticity and a keen awareness of our true self. Unsure of who we really are we put on masks created by others and we struggle to conform to their expectations in order to gain acceptance. Like us, however, they too are in search of their true selves and the images we have made of each other are only projections of our own insecurities.

The false sense of self this has created makes genuine acceptance of oneself and others painfully unattainable. Severed from the source of true love, we enter into relationships to find intimacy; we hope, expect, and even demand that the other fulfill our longings and deepest needs. We try desperately to make it work, positioning our "second love" as our "first love," only to find ourselves broken hearted and disillusioned.

Our chameleon-like existence and self-gratifying relationships cannot fulfill our fervent desire to be reunited with our first love, the source of our true self and our true home. We feel unsettled and restless, constantly searching, or we settle for the next best thing. We surge ahead and cling so tightly to imitations that can only offer momentary relief. We even deceive ourselves into believing that second best is all that we can have. We are left wanting more, restless and determined to find the cure for our ailing soul. In this reactive pattern, we become accustomed to relying on external cues or voices as aids in navigating our interior landscape. These voices and reactive gestures, however, prevent us from hearing and responding to the inner voice of love, which comes as a gentle whisper.

We cannot resolve this dilemma by force, but by quiet and stillness. In this posture, we learn how to look deeply, listening intently and inwardly to both our experience of exile and the attendant longing for communion. Our inner looking and listening makes us aware of that primordial reality where homesickness is foreign and the at home feeling of being in the presence of God permeates. Until then we remain ill at ease and lost, and the experience of true communion and union with ourselves, others, and God is but a faint memory and a distant hope.

HUMAN SUFFERING

Constricted by our finitude, driven by restlessness, and induced by unfulfilled longings we go about our lives in frantic search of our true home, true love, and true identity. We cling to ideas, people, experiences, relationships, or professional identities that we hoped would fill the gaping hole within us. The cycle of restlessness, reaction, and rapaciousness is the breeding ground of human suffering. The creation narrative exposes this daunting yet redeemable reality.

Despite, according to Genesis 2, being quickened to life by God's own breath, being given a bountiful supply of food, and being put in charge of the garden, the man whom God created from the dust of the ground felt incomplete and lonely. God recognized this dilemma and declared: "It is not good for the man to be alone" (2:18), and woman was created. The Genesis narrative points to the fundamental human experience of aloneness. But that is not all. The creature, though bearing the image of the Creator, is a finite being and therefore limited in all ways. Though endowed with the necessary faculties to both survive and thrive, ontologically humankind cannot exceed the limits of finitude. The limits of creaturely being are symbolized by the fruit-bearing tree at the center of the garden, the desire for which is a mark of resistance against human finitude.[1]

The refusal to accept the conditions and limits of finite existence renders the archetypal beings vulnerable to temptation. Divine love and communion did not satisfy Adam and Eve any longer. Instead, they were distracted and held captive by their desire not just to be like God, but to be God themselves. The tempter took advantage of this opportunity by inducing doubt in them (Gen 3:1) and magnifying their seething desire to be someone other than who they were created to be. Convinced that they could be more, they grasped onto the false longing to be like God (3:6) and eventually crossed the point of no return. Sin entered and like a virus infected all of creation.

Often I see myself doing exactly what the primordial couple did in the garden. The constant urge to cave in to selfish desires and intentions, doubt as to the sufficiency of God, and reliance on my own knowledge and skills, productivity, and self-importance are so ingrained it is often hard to prevent their influence in everything that I do. When convicted of such hubris, the initial impulse is not repentance or a desire to lay bare before the Lord a contrite heart, but rationalization, denial, or a shifting of blame to others.

The act of self-assertion replaces "first love" with estrangement and the compulsion to be in control. In the Genesis narrative, being-for-oneself, or self-indulgence and self-possession, becomes the driving force of the couple's existence. Stringing leaves to cover their nakedness becomes a compelling representation of their attempt to self-manage the outcome of their disobedience. In this narrative, God's experience of rest is counter to the experience of restlessness that emanates from the conditions of human finitude, which include being alone and lonely, limited, and prone to temptation.[2] Out of these anxious feelings comes a reaction, an aggressive gesture that results in their transgression of God's command and intentions for them. Confronted by what they have done, they cling to each other and hide themselves from the presence and companionship of God. Such estrangement sires suffering of many kinds. Yet at the root of all this is the refusal both to accept their utter dependence and to trust the sufficiency of God in all of life, which is the heart of true communion and union.

PROCESS OF CHANGE

The creation narrative is also a continuing story of redemption and an invitation to return to a life of communion and union with God the Creator. The wilful attempt of the couple to cover their sin is matched with the mindful and intentional action of God to redeem them (3:21). Despite their disobedience and eventual separation, God remains committed to them as symbolized by the garment of skin God used not just to cover their shame, but to clothe them, a visual reminder of God's indestructible love and unbreakable connection with them (Rom 8:39). In the midst of betrayed love, God, out of love, restores, protects, and reconnects with them as symbolized by the garment of skin, a foreshadowing of the ultimate expression of God's love to all humanity through the incarnation of Jesus Christ (Is 61:10; Rom 3:22).

Though we are marred by the distorting effects of sin and the sinful choices we have made, we are held together by God's ongoing act of redemption. God's display of utter regard for our well-being is a lure toward this restful place where our primary posture is not self-mastery or self-assertion but surrender, submission, and self-transcendence. Put another way, the disorientation that separation brings is not the final story. Love is both the beginning and end of the story. Deep in our hearts there is a seed of contemplation, a thirst for an intimate connection with God, a longing to return to the love from which we came.

There is no other place where human suffering and the potential for change and transformation are more acutely examined than in counseling. The stories told in this shared space are replete with evidence of the fundamental human problem of estrangement or alienation.

Estrangement has many names, including depression, anxiety, addiction, and domestic violence, and it can thwart the potential for a transformed life if left unattended. Estrangement does not discriminate and knows no boundaries; it is both personal and universal at the same time. Although estrangement is ubiquitous, the potential for healing and change remains. Counseling offers a space where estrangement can be addressed and transformed. The counselor's contemplative stance is critical in converting the potential for healing into an actual experience of the transformed life that clients seek.

> *Having spent a week in silent retreat, I went back to the office the following Monday with a full case load waiting for me. As I briefly glanced at my schedule, the words in Isaiah 40:1-2 came to mind: "Comfort, comfort, my people, says your God. Speak tenderly to Jerusalem, and proclaim to her that her hard service has been completed, that her sin has been paid for, that she has received from the Lord's hand double for all her sins." Right there at that moment the tone of the day was set and an attitude of surrender to the Great Comforter was evoked within me. The experience of silence, peace, focused attention, and widening expanse that I experienced the previous week came over me and stayed with me as I sat and met with each of my clients that day.*

The contemplative counselor's dedicated and regular cultivation of his or her interior garden prepares him or her to engage in the therapeutic process with clients in a manner that is supportive of and enhances the experience of healing and transformation.

FOCUSED AND BARE ATTENTION

Paying close attention to the client's unfolding experience in the here and now does not always come easy for either novice or seasoned therapists. Our wandering minds often take us out of the present moment and into our residual past (for example, lingering conflicts that have arisen recently in our personal lives) or anticipated future (such as strategies to fend off feelings of dread and anxiety caused by these unresolved conflicts). Sometimes we may find the materials that our clients present in therapy either boring or too threatening and evocative of our own unresolved issues, and so we end up tuning them out. Or we may be so consumed by our own felt sense of inadequacy or perfectionism that we swirl around in our heads rehearsing or hunting for the right question or response to give our unsuspecting clients. We pursue every thought or feeling that comes to mind and camouflage our inattention by asking seemingly probing questions or making comments such as "say more." Our clients' experience of invalidation, of not being seen or heard or taken seriously in his or her familiar world, is re-enacted once again in the consulting room due to our inaccessible and inattentive presence.

The sustained practice of mindfulness strengthens the counselor's ability to engage in two equally important forms of attention, each pivotal in the practice of psychotherapy, namely focused attention and bare attention. As the name implies, focused attention is about directing all of one's awareness onto a single object to the exclusion of everything else. The practice of mindful breathing is an example of this type of invested attention.

The practice of mindful breathing enhances the counselor's ability to remain narrowly focused on the client when practicing psychotherapy. Everything recedes into the background and the client takes center stage in the mind of the counselor. Mindful breathing grounds the counselor in the present moment with the client and quickens his or her spirit to stay engaged and fully awake to the task at hand. This focused attention that clients receive from the counselor generates feelings of being seen, heard, and validated, thus providing a corrective emotional experience that is lacking in most of their relationships. This fosters trust in the therapeutic relationship and confidence in its power to facilitate healing. When distracting thoughts or feelings surface, the counselor who has a developed capacity to be fully present is able to observe and notice what occurs in his or her mind without getting caught in it. Becoming mindful of one's breathing whenever the mind wanders anchors the counselor to the present and promotes attentiveness and alertness.

As counselors continue to devote personal time to harnessing their capacity to be fully present in the here and now, they soon discover how rich and textured their lives really are. A sense of curiosity, even a sense of wonder over what used to be considered ordinary and trivial, begins to grow. With this new attitude comes a new way of approaching every moment of their lives; each is experienced as a gift to be unwrapped with keen interest and attention. When clients are encountered in this manner, they begin to feel important, connected, and acknowledged for who they really are: a precious gift, a bearer of God's image, God's own beloved.

Bare or panoramic attention is the capacity to become evenly aware of not just one object but of all things, of what is happening internally and relationally between counselor and client. The counselor is a participant observer, engaging and making genuine contact and connection with the client while remaining attentive and "flexible with whatever is in the field of perception."[3] This capacity allows the counselor to monitor the relational dynamics occurring in the consulting room moment by moment and to make necessary adjustments to optimize the transforming power of *being with*.

This "choiceless awareness"[4] prepares the counselor to tune in and discern the presence and prompting of God in their midst. The on-going practice of silence and solitude poises the counselor to engage in a dialogue with God, which, according to Swiss physician Paul Tornier, who is known for his work in pastoral counseling, runs parallel with the dialogue that is happening between the counselor and client. He writes:

> There are two parallel dialogues, two personal contacts—one with another person, the other with God . . . for the words which are exchanged between my patient and me have no significance apart from the inner movement of the soul which is taking place within

us both and which is at this moment, for me as well as for him, personal contact with God. That is why at that moment silence can be even more valuable than words.[5]

The ability to move fluidly between focused attention and bare attention is what the contemplative counselor strives for. Psychotherapy needs both levels of awareness given the dynamic nature of the therapeutic relationship. By tuning in solely to the client moment by moment, the counselor solidifies identification and deepens understanding of and connection with the client. Bare attention with its feelings of "impartiality, of spaciousness, of breadth of vision,"[6] evokes both flexibility and freedom in choosing which healing paths to take.

HOSPITABLE RECEPTION

From a contemplative perspective, counseling is conceived of as a sacred therapeutic space where clients can come and be treated as guests. This hospitable reception invites clients to unload their heavy burdens, to fall apart, to have someone witness the depth of their pain and brokenness in a rhythm that is neither hurried nor forced.

Carl came to therapy to deal with feeling rejected and disrespected by his peers and close friends. He seemed uncomfortable and vague when asked to describe a recent incident that conjured up such strong reactions. He was very cautious and deliberate in his choice of words, as if not wanting to know or hear his own story or have it be known by me. Instead of pressing for more information or interpreting his reluctance or sharing with him my observations, I opted to honor and respect his cadence and let him direct our time together. Toward the end of our session, he told me that he still has a lot of stuff that he would like to talk to me about next time. I smiled and ushered him out of the office.

The counselor's experience of security in his or her identity as the beloved of God, accepted and loved unconditionally, removes the unnecessary pressure to perform, produce results, or make an impression. Grounded in this secure base, I can now venture outward and extend that same level of unreserved acceptance to someone like Carl who is in search of a home base where he will feel connected and acknowledged. My first gesture of hospitality is an open and welcoming stance toward whatever unfolds in the present moment with him; I neither direct nor impose, but simply make myself available and accessible to him as he journeys toward self-discovery.

A contemplative and mindful stance expands the counselor's interiority so that clients can come and inhabit a safe space, rest their weary hearts and catch their breath. In this relaxed and serene state, I was able to offer Carl a holding environment where he could find his own rhythm and become acquainted with his own grief and sorrows without much external impingement. In an experiential and symbolical manner, he was invited to let things be as they were according to what felt safe and comfortable for him at that time. This is the essence of hospitality: a receptive and open invitation to Carl to come just as he is and be welcomed, acknowledged, and respected. Such hospitality sparks trust so that Carl can begin to open up and risk being known by me.

What clients experience as welcoming and honoring relationally can be extended personally to the way they respond to their own emotional lives. It is far too common for clients to hide from or hold onto their suffering without realizing that such defensive responses move them deeper into a quagmire of despair and hopelessness. The soft, hospitable, and calm approach I took with Carl implied that he could adopt an accepting and non-judgmental stance toward himself and his ways of dealing with his own suffering. Any premature interpretation, challenge, or observation on my part could have sent the message that his suffering was so overwhelming for him that it required immediate intervention from me as his therapist. Such a course of action would imply that I had already made a judgment with regard to his incapacity to tolerate his own suffering. More so, it would have revealed my own discomfort in sitting with him in his dark hour.

Conversely, Carl's experience of hospitality in that shared space released his potential to extend that same level of acceptance and non-judgment to his own subjective experience. The stable and secure space I tried to foster during our time together, even when he was reluctant and evasive, communicated my readiness to embrace all of him and all of his experiences. His tendency to hide from himself and me was both acknowledged and validated, leading to a growing desire to open up and let someone into his life. As he continues to experience this hospitable reception in our time together, he becomes less reactive and more pro-active in extending acceptance and hospitality to his subjective life experiences, thus replacing their power to intimidate and induce fear with a new readiness to be transformed.

FLEXIBLE CONCEPTUALIZATION

There are a myriad of approaches to psychotherapy available to us in our work with clients. The proliferation of these models affords us the ability to tailor our intervention strategies to meet the unique needs of our clients. This, of course, presupposes a depth of knowledge and understanding of these various explanatory models and an accurate assessment of the client's presenting problem. When done in collaboration, the process of change clients go through demonstrates the efficacy of psychotherapy in alleviating and transforming human suffering.

However, despite access to these resources, there is still a tendency to rely on our own default or preferred theory in guiding the therapeutic process. This "infatuation with theory"[7] inhibits personal and genuine contact with clients and renders them as objects to be studied rather than persons to be encountered. When this happens, we inadvertently pigeon-hole clients to fit our theoretical mold, thereby denying their complexity and dishonouring their uniqueness as human beings.

The contemplative stance of non-attachment and mindful reception and openness to the novelty of the present moment releases the counselor from the tendency to hold tightly onto a particular theoretical model in conducting psychotherapy. This creates an opportunity for an on-going and collaborative discernment process with clients who are seen as active participants in determining the process and outcome of their healing journey. To hold onto these models lightly is to acknowledge the provisional nature of all theories. They serve as guideposts that illumine our path as we seek to become competent and effective therapists, and must point us in the direction of a more nuanced description and understanding of the whole person with whom we are working.

Integral to a life of contemplation is tolerance toward or gracious acceptance of unknowing and not knowing. Our regular descent into our interior garden in silence and solitude to be with God involves waiting upon him and in that state we consent to suspend our desire both to be in control and to know. The clenched fists that come with trying to be in control give way to open palms ready to wait and to trust in God who knows.

Comfort with not knowing is essential to a contemplative practice of counseling. Instead of letting our mind wander or theorize about our client's problems, which steals us from the present moment, we tune in to a level of therapeutic encounter that is beyond discursive thinking. This does not mean abandoning our clinical training, experience, and what we have to offer as therapists. It simply means learning to "cling less firmly to imagined certainty, and to trust that an open and attuned mind (fortified by firm clinical training) will be far more responsive to the demands of the moment than one resting on concepts alone. It grants us access to all the tools at our disposal, based on the genuine needs of the present, and allows us the freedom to jettison them when they are unhelpful."[8]

It would have been a lot easier for me to adopt a psychological theory that would help explain and possibly ease Carl's struggle to cope with experiences of rejection and loneliness. I have dealt with similar situations before and have used evidenced-based treatments that have been proven effective in dealing with issues of self-worth and interpersonal challenges. As helpful as this might have been, I decided simply to keep an open mind and allow the ebb and flow of silence and sound to dictate what needed to happen next.

Though the impulse was there to ask questions to fill in the gaps that Carl had left, I managed somehow to tame it and let the present moment evolve the way it would. There was no rush to know; instead I accepted the reality of not knowing and rested in the assurance that everything has its own rhythm and timing. Focused attention and hospitable reception to all events in the therapeutic process were salient attributes in discovering the unique rhythm of our work together.

EMPATHY AND COMPASSION

Tornier describes psychotherapy as a "relationship in dialogue,"[9] and in this encounter a deep connection between counselor and client is inevitable. Though roles are clearly defined, the atmosphere of hospitality and dialogue that contemplative based counseling attempts to foster opens up the possibility for the dyad to mutually impact each other in significant ways. For the counselor, this may mean permitting the story and life of the client to touch his or her own being and narrative, resulting in the realization that counselor and client are far more alike than they are different. For the client, it may mean allowing the counselor to enter into his or her internal, private world and, through that process, experience faithful accompaniment in the journey toward healing.

The experience of shared humanity is advanced and maintained by the counselor's empathic and compassionate connection with his or her clients. Empathy allows the counselor to get a glimpse of the client's interior world. Through empathy, the counselor "inhabits" the client's interior world as fully as he or she can in order to gain understanding while remaining personally grounded. The "as if"[10] quality inherent in this relational encounter strengthens the identification process of sharing or experiencing the feelings of the client, which is the hallmark of empathy. For this to happen, the counselor needs to fully attend to the client's unfolding experience in the here and now and tune in ever so faithfully and accurately to their subjective shifts. Such focused attention is the product of disciplined mindfulness practices that a contemplative counselor undertakes in his or her personal life.

Empathic attunement expands the counselor's ability "to relax, mentally and spiritually, as well as physically, learning to let one's self go into the other person with a willingness to be changed in the process."[11] Carl's apparent reticence to disclose his story speaks to the human tendency to hide ourselves from unpleasant and painful experiences. Yet, he has also shown a readiness to deal with his suffering differently, as evidenced by his decision to participate in therapy. As I accept his conflicted feelings with curiosity, our relational bonds and the safety of the relational space are strengthened. My openness to be changed or impacted by Carl nourishes the gift of compassion that I extend toward him.

Compassion involves being open to, aware, and accepting of our own suffering, our own humanity. A life of contemplation helps "to change our relationship to suffering by surrendering our need to reject it. This is an act of kindness to oneself. Our own suffering offers an opportunity to become openhearted rather than merely oppressed.[12] Suffering is all around us and it often brings us to our knees in acknowledgment of both our limitations and our great need for the grace of God if we are to endure and be transformed by suffering (2 Cor 12:9). The notion of a completely separate self is dismantled by the offering of compassion, by the counselor's willingness to suffer with those who suffer, not out of altruistic motives, but from a pure experience of his or her "innate affinity with all beings."[13]

Indeed, I experienced an affinity or identification with Carl in terms of both the human tendency to reject suffering and the human potential to surrender to it. I was mindful of and understood quite well his defensive maneuvering as he attempted to run away from his suffering. As I modeled for him a hospitable stance toward all of his experiences, unpleasant or pleasant, he developed the potential to extend grace and kindness toward himself.

EQUANIMITY

The stable, impartial, and open-minded stance the counselor inhabits when listening deeply to the client is an example of equanimity. In the mindfulness tradition, equanimity is understood in two ways. First, equanimity describes a "non-discriminating, open receptivity in which all experience is welcome."[14] Nothing is deemed as unfruitful or trivial, and everything is treated with the same level of curiosity and hospitality. Carl's tendency to both conceal and reveal his story was met with an unbiased stance. I was neither impatient with his inhibition nor excited when he promised to reveal more in the next session. In other words, I tried to provide an "evenly hovering attention . . . or a posture of nearness to each moment within the therapeutic process,"[15] which deepened my connection and attunement to Carl's subjective shifts. Empathy flourishes when equanimity is achieved in therapy.

Second, equanimity also connotes acceptance of the limits of our therapeutic intentions and involvement in the healing process of our clients.[16] Ultimately, the promise of change lies in the client's own motivation and willingness to take ownership of and responsibility for their own flourishing as a human being. It is far too common for clients to expect counselors to wave their therapeutic wand and miraculously bring about change and healing. In fact, we sometimes collude with them by performing as well-skilled technicians, mapping intervention strategies to relieve them of their suffering. Consequently, we miss the opportunity to model for them what it would mean for them to become fully present to their own suffering, without rejecting or grasping, but by simply attending to it wholeheartedly.

Equanimity "allows us to stop trying to fix things long enough to see what is."[17] By helping clients to stay and look deeply into their suffering, the counselor helps them both to discover their innate resilience in the face of life's inevitable trials and to realize that they are really much stronger than they think.

CROSS

The contemplative approach to change and transformation targets the core problem of estrangement and the reactive stance of attachment and avoidance. It does this by fostering *c*uriosity, *r*eceptivity, *o*penness, *s*tillness, and *s*urrender—CROSS. This acronym is a heuristic device designed to help counselors frame their personal and clinical presence within the context of the contemplative tradition as outlined above.

The cross, as a concrete visual image, enjoins the counselor to engage in the on-going practice of self-emptying as he or she assumes the posture of service through the faithful stewardship of his or her gifts and graces (Phil 2:7). The stretched out arms of the cross are a powerful representation of the counselor's relational stance toward the client and the process of psychotherapy—self-emptying, attentive, and accessible.

As a framework, CROSS is dynamic, interactive, and interdependent—not linear or one-dimensional. It is an emblem of the counselor's intention to provide an alternative experience of psychotherapy, one where the counselor's primary posture is to *be with* the client, contemplatively and mindfully.

Curiosity is an off-shoot of being awake and alert in the present moment. All events in therapy are received with an equal measure of hovering and bare attention, all are subject to the same level of curious knowing and exploration. The spirit of inquisitiveness stalls the tendency of counselors to judge experiences that evolve in therapy as good or bad. All too often, sessions are considered good and exciting when there is movement toward the client's desired therapeutic goal and bad or difficult when the reverse happens. This mirrors the conditioned response of aversion toward unpleasant experiences and attachment to pleasant ones, which contemplation and mindfulness seek to transform, partly through the attitude of curiosity.

Receptivity renders the counselor psychologically available and accessible both to the client's unfolding experience and to the vicissitudes of the psychotherapeutic process. The steady, focused, and non-judgmental reception of the client's thoughts and feelings during the course of therapy provides a different experience, especially for those who are mired in self-hate and self-blame. This corrective relational experience often surprises clients, but a consistent display of such unconditional hospitality softens their hardened and fearful heart and brings them to a place where they can begin to love themselves and others again. All this, of course, is significantly dependent on the counselor's own level of self-acceptance and kindness toward him or herself. Sometimes counselors are their own worst critic, and often the drive to perform and succeed is a way of both taming the harsh inner judge and stilling the nagging sense of not being good enough. However, so long as the counselor practices unconditional positive regard toward him or herself on the basis of an experiential knowledge of God's love for him or her, accepting clients as they are inevitably ensues.

Openness to the freshness that the present moment brings is essential to a contemplative practice of counseling. This does not mean abandoning all previous therapeutic work so that the therapeutic dyad can start anew every session. It simply means holding previous therapeutic work lightly enough to leave room for whatever occurs in the moment. The confluence of work that has already been done and work that is yet to be done occurs when counselor and client are engaged fully in the present therapeutic moment. Being together and attentive to what unfolds in the present moment, affords greater freedom and flexibility to explore and pursue that which will bring about lasting change and transformation for the client.

Openness also prepares the counselor to be impacted by the client and the experience of participating in the healing process. Counseling is an intimate and powerful experience with the potential to leave both client and counselor changed and transformed.

Stillness within supports and makes possible the relational stance of curiosity, reception, openness, and surrender. It emerges from a deep and abiding conviction that God is present in the therapeutic space, that faithful stewardship of one's counseling skills and knowledge re-orients one's focus and intention, and that the therapeutic relationship takes a curative turn when one attempts simply to be fully present with one's client. Imbued by these convictions, the counselor approaches the task from a place of inner peace and equanimity. He or she is neither perturbed nor unsettled by the ebb and flow of the counseling process, but remains fully awake and engaged in all that transpires in the room. His or her non-anxious presence becomes an open invitation to the client to be his or her authentic self.

Surrender is about releasing control and the need to control and learning to accept aspects of the therapeutic work that are unknown or yet to be known. There is so much to know about therapy, about the person with whom we are working, about who we are as counselors, about God, who hallows the therapeutic space, and all that can be missed if we are unable to relinquish the need for control and mastery. By holding tightly to our theories, our techniques, our agenda and carefully planned strategies, we end up stifling the freedom, creativity, and courage needed to break new ground and discover new ways of being in therapy. And yet, when we surrender all that we are to God, to the therapeutic process itself, to the gift of the present moment, we realize all the more the richness and textured quality of human experience and human relationships.

VINCENT'S VIRTUES AND VICES

Vincent is a twenty-five-year old single man who has been wrestling with anxiety most of his life. He appeared somewhat distraught and ruffled when he showed up for our initial session. After a brief introduction we both sat in silence for a little while. Then tears started to stream down his face, and in that moment I witnessed the depth of his pain. Being mindful of what was happening in the moment, in him, in me, and between the two of us, I remained non-anxious and receptive. There was an urge within me to inquire into what the tears meant, but thankfully I restrained myself and waited.

Soon he started to mumble, which I took as a signal that he was ready to express in words what his body, through tears, was trying to convey. What followed was the telling of a story filled with experiences of rejection and abandonment, uncertainty and self-doubt, of broken promises, dreams, and relationships.

Vincent grew up with an alcoholic father who deserted him and his mother when Vincent was eight years old. Having to fend for themselves, they shuttled from one place to another and relied on other people just to survive. His mother hooked up with another man who turned out to be as abusive as his biological father. The psychic wounds inflicted upon him early festered, leaving him in despair, unsure of himself, and uncertain about the future. He then turned to drugs and alcohol to calm his nerves, to numb his pain, and to escape from the harsh reality of his life. He works just to get by, to keep himself distracted, and to support his habits. His relationships are sparse, tentative, and often awkward. Increasingly, he is becoming more withdrawn and his anxiety is intensifying. The discomfort this brings him led him to my office.

BEING WITH VINCENT

Mindful attending in counseling is critical. Contemplation as a way of life begets a markedly transforming way of being in therapy. The effect of regular rhythms of silence, stillness, and solitude of the heart in daily life foster an attitude of mindfulness or watchfulness in professional life. As a therapeutic stance, my primary intent is to *be with* Vincent, always *curious* in a non-intrusive way, mindfully attending or noticing the shifts, the whispers, the spoken words, or the subtle longings he is expressing as they occur in the moment. This restful, unhurried, and hospitable approach opens the door for him to stay in therapy in all his glory and goriness.

The gracious act of focused and bare attention and the acceptance that we extend our clients emanate from accepting ourselves as God's beloved and being mindful of our own subjective reality. Silence and solitude prepare the ground of the heart to be focused and accepting.

Journeying with Vincent requires the creation of a space where his anxiety is honored, not by soothing it quickly through various interpretive moves or grand techniques, but by letting him be as he is. His anxiety must be countered by tranquility, his seemingly disordered self-presentation received with hospitality. To do this, I need to inhabit and reflect a quiet and peaceful presence myself and not be swayed by my tendency for quick action and resolution. The regular practice of mindful breathing and silence both in and outside of the consulting room expands my capacity for bare attention and my awareness of the present moment in all its texture and nuanced manifestations. In mindful breathing, for example, my body, mind, and spirit are held together in a harmony that grounds me in the present moment so that I can attune to Vincent's unfolding experience. Interior silence makes possible the sharpening of the "third ear"[18] so that I can listen to his story, spoken freely or intimated subtlety, and discern with clarity words and gestures that betray his outer and inner disposition.

This hospitable *reception* is a gentle invitation for Vincent to inhabit the space he is in as he is, without restrictions or impingement. The experience of equanimity solidifies empathy and genuine connection, which leads to Vincent beginning to feel both felt and seen, and honored and received completely. This is critical in a number of ways. Through a non-demanding presence, the counselor is able to see the client's "uninterrupted flow of authentic self."[19] The counselor's *open* and non-judging stance invites the client to fall apart or experience the constantly evolving flow of his or her emotions and thoughts, without any hurried interpretations and interventions. The counselor just lets the client be.

Vincent's ongoing struggle with anxiety is partly a result of avoidance tactics that he clings to when unresolved issues of his painful past surface. Immobilized and tormented by the piercing ache of rejection and abandonment experienced early in his life, he reaches for the bottle to numb the pain, only to find himself stung by that pain again and again. As a consequence, his anxiety follows him like a shadow and takes the form of restlessness, obsessive thinking, and outbursts of anger and despondency.

From a contemplative standpoint, the attitude of *stillness* that seeks no action except to be fully present with oneself and with another in the unfolding of connection—without interruption, judgment, or quick solution—exemplifies a markedly different relationship toward suffering. This relationship is characterized by hospitality, and not hostility, toward suffering. The steady and non-reactive stance of the counselor gives clients the opportunity to relate to their suffering differently. As they continue to experience the counselor in this manner, they begin to realize, either directly or indirectly, that acceptance and not avoidance is what makes them acutely aware of their finitude and open to the infinite possibilities inherent in suffering for reframing and transforming their lives.

Vincent began to learn how to attend non-judgingly to his subjective experience as it unfolds in the moment, however painful, bewildering, and debilitating as it may be. The avoidance that he was accustomed to practicing, when either suddenly or gradually hit by the lingering memories of his past, began to give way as he learned to remain present to his thoughts, emotions, and bodily responses in the presence of another. Vincent's willingness to descend to places where it hurts the most, his courage to be, is a testament to his resilience and a vivid reminder to himself that he is not alone in his suffering.

Suffering with the client is characteristic of a contemplative, mindful approach to counseling. The hospitable reception and companionship the counselor provides for his or her clients in their deep and darkest hour is a visible and compelling embodiment of what it means to suffer with them, the true definition of compassion.

Bearing witness to Vincent's struggles, without judgment or hasty moves to cure, bridges the gap and isolation that suffering brings. Indeed, suffering had created a chasm between Vincent and his immediate world. Protecting himself from potential psychic injury, he learned to hide his pain from himself and others, leaving him feeling more and more abandoned and disconnected.

The simple act of my being *mindfully present* as his counselor acknowledged Vincent's conflicted feelings regarding self-disclosure and invited him to take the risk of letting someone in. He is beginning to realize that he is not alone and he does not have to detach himself from his own subjectivity. He can now begin to let his repressed thoughts and feelings emerge, recognize them for what they are and, with an attitude of curiosity, unearth the treasure hidden in the cracked vessel of his storied life. In other words, as Vincent learns to de-identify or de-center himself from his thoughts and feelings and painful past and fears, his shadow self disappears and his true self emerges. With the flourishing of the true self come multiple possibilities to deal with the ghosts of the past that have haunted him for so long and prevented him from living fully in the present.

To suffer with also means letting the pain of another touch our own fundamental brokenness and pain. Empathy is not just about entering the world of another to gain deeper understanding of what they are going through. Through empathy we discover that we are more alike than different. The experience of our shared humanity deepens empathic attunement, connection, and compassion. Like Vincent, I have also regarded suffering as an enemy to be avoided or conquered through the weapons of work, accomplishments, even relationships. I have also cocooned myself and restricted others from seeing that part of me that is vulnerable and afraid, all the while still longing to be accepted and loved. Empathy, understood in this manner, is the great equalizer between counselor and client in that, even though the relationship is asymmetrical due to our unique roles in counselling, we discover that we both are equally subject to human finitude and divine grace. In other words, though we have charted two different paths, Vincent and I are cut from same cloth for we both suffer from the fundamental problem of estrangement and we are both objects of unmerited love and grace. Since my humanity is intertwined with his own, his liberation and healing are also connected to mine. The relationship that develops out of our shared humanity is a potent balm for the healing of his psychic wound; the act of solidarity displayed in this relationship makes possible the experience of an authentic human connection.

In the privacy of my devotional life, I have also become increasingly more aware that fundamentally Vincent and I are bound together in love and for love, and that in faith and before the throne of grace we are invited to cast all our anxieties on God who cares for the wounded and wearied (1 Pt 5:7; see also Mt 6). We are both in need of and subject to divine grace; therapy is a way of specifically extending this grace to him. The human-to-human connection is real and authentic, but no less clinical and therapeutic. In fact, this genuine encounter has been a critical aspect of Vincent's healing journey.

Individuals like Vincent (including myself) suffer a great deal primarily because of over identification with thoughts, feelings, and behavior. Often, we find ourselves being tossed to and fro by the strong current or wave of our emotional and mental life. Unquestioned beliefs about ourselves, others and the world keep playing in our head like a broken record. The intensity of our emotional reactions only gains strength as we identify ourselves endlessly with our self-talk and unedited narrative. Having lost our grip on our internal processes, we react automatically and mindlessly, which results in various forms of emotional dysregulation (such as depression and anxiety) along with cognitive distortion, and relational ruptures.

Generally in counseling, the opportunity to pause or drop into stillness is a rare occurrence. The awkward feeling silence generates, especially when we stumble on it unintentionally, sets off an instinctual need to fill the space with words and gestures. Hence, talk therapy still dominates and silence in therapy is more the exception than the rule. Inadvertently, we miss the opportunity to help our clients discover their capacity for contemplative, mindful existence.

When we approach the task of counseling from a contemplative and mindful stance, we help clients begin to settle into or ground themselves in the present moment. This shifts their attention away from worries about the future over which they have no control whatsoever or depressing events from the past, which can never be undone. When the client is rehashing the past or rehearsing the future, he or she misses the gift that the present moment brings, which is all there is. Inviting clients to return to where they are in actuality, in the consulting room with the counsellor, also disentangles them from the automatic thought patterns, emotional reactions, and reflexive responses they are conditioned to grasp onto.

Stepping back to witness what is happening subjectively is critical to the change process. Silence moves the client from reactivity to response-ability. They are no longer lost in the whirlwind of their thoughts and emotions, but instead are gaining competency in regulating them.

Vincent learned to be mindful of his interior life both during and after our sessions together. During therapy, Vincent was encouraged to let himself experience and identify the flow of emotions and thoughts that were surfacing. Giving him ample time to go inward to witness what was happening in his interior life was critical in our work together. There was no need for either of us to rush the process. Instead, he was encouraged to remain open, hospitable, and non-judgemental to the unfolding of his subjective life. Sharing what he discovered in his descent inward became more natural and free-flowing over time. As a counselor, all that I had to do at that time was to listen quietly, occasionally prompting him to continue on the path of self-discovery. There was no probing for more or offering of interpretations; I just let the flow of his subjectivity be as it was without forced re-descriptions. With awareness of and hospitality to his interior life came the dawning of self-acceptance, and a gracious acknowledgement of his complexity, beauty, and profundity.

The distance created between self and experience through mindfulness practice grounded in *curiosity, receptivity, openness, stillness, and surrender* (CROSS) has allowed Vincent to look at himself and his situation from multiple vantage points. No longer imprisoned by rigidity and reactivity, he has gradually discerned some aspects of his narrative that need to be re-written (or worked through) and some that can be tossed in the wind.

In this process of discernment, Vincent also became increasingly aware of his own spiritual impulses hidden beneath his avoidance of and attachment to suffering. As he descended deeper into his interior garden, he felt more at peace, accompanied, and deeply loved. The rediscovery of that sacred space in his heart led him to remember instances in his life when he had felt close to God, first through the example of his mother's faith and then by his own experiences of God's presence. Once again, I was led to honor his disclosure by simply listening, letting "deep call to deep" (Ps 42:7) as the Spirit of God enfolded Vincent's spirit in the dance of healing and re-birth.

Subsequent sessions with Vincent were edifying experiences for both of us. He showed up at these meetings with a smile on his face, excited to share what it was like to live in the moment without the burdens of the past and worries of the future. From time to time he would come with residual concerns, not with foreboding fear or paralysing anxiety, but with courage and a peaceful countenance. Tears still flowed and memories of a painful past still surfaced, but his attitude toward these moments had changed. No longer hiding from or numbing his pain, Vincent reported becoming more careful and intentional in his lifestyle choices and open and receptive to people around him. Finally, he found himself listening to that still, small, and gentle voice of God, showing him the path of healing and transformation.

The experience of being fully encountered and accepted in all of his humanity gave Vincent a sense of self-agency along with the belief that he need not travel on his journey alone. He has accepted God's invitation for communion and union, an invitation that can be nurtured interiorly in prayer, silence, and solitude and exteriorly through meaningful relationships and mutual accompaniment with others.

Reflecting on the journey with Vincent has been a humbling experience. His pain touched the pain in my own heart and his healing became the balm for my own soul-ache. We are both created in the image of God, both subjected to the problem of estrangement, and both still on the journey toward God, our true home.

Chapter 5

CHRISTIAN CONTEMPLATION: A WAY OF ACTION

> Each hour of the day we should note and weigh our actions
> and in the evening we should do what we can
> to free ourselves of the burden by means of repentance—
> if, that is, we wish, with God's help to overcome wickedness.
> We should also make sure that we perform all our outward tasks
> in a manner that accords with God's will, before God and for God alone.
>
> *St. Hesychios the Priest*

In the gospel of Matthew, we see Jesus withdrawing to a solitary place when he heard of John the Baptist's murder by King Herod (Mt 14:13ff). Jesus retreated to the desert to be alone with God. When people heard of Jesus' whereabouts, they followed him on foot, and when he saw them, "he had compassion on them and healed their sick" (14). There are three significant movements in this narrative: (1) he saw them (attention), (2) he felt compassion for them (intention), and (3) he healed those who needed healing (action). The movement of attention, intention, and action reveals a pattern that is also common to those who practice the contemplative life.

Jesus' devotion to and unity with God reveals a heart that is undivided, attentive, and dedicated to the accomplishment of God's will on earth. The self-giving and loving nature of God in Jesus Christ allowed him to see people as they truly are, like sheep without a shepherd. Looking deeply into the hearts of people engendered not pity or sympathy, but a deep and abiding compassion for them. The suffering of people moved his heart profoundly and compelled him to action.

Such is the nature of God's love, always attentive, bearing the fruit of compassion, concrete, and incarnational. The incarnation of God in Jesus Christ is a clear and radical testament to God's lavish love. As a fruit of love, compassion is the willingness to suffer with those who suffer and, through tangible words and deeds, provide relief for their suffering. Compassion is a willingness to "run the risk of suffering with and for the beloved. . . . Once we choose to live our lives with compassion, we then live ready to embrace the probability that our loving will bring us face to face with suffering."[1]

In contemplative spirituality, being encountered and embraced by God Alone in prayer, silence, and solitude (attention) heals our spiritual blindness and lets us see truly and deeply the true condition of ourselves and others. Though cracked and broken, we as earthen vessels carry the divine light of God that illumines our nature as cre-ated for and by love. This divine love is both diffusive and self-giving, and so thrusts us toward others with empathy and compassion (inten-tion). The fruit of compassion is love expressed concretely, visibly, and incarnationally through the alleviation and transformation of human suffering (action).

The singular and continuous movement of descending inward to be in communion with God and ascending outward to be with God's people is at the core of contemplative action. The internal gazing upon God heightens one's awareness of the principalities and powers that overtly or subtly stifle freedom, stall the development of a critical consciousness, and inhibit the potential we all have to engage in the active pursuit of personal and societal transformation. In other words, the contemplative life reorients our perspectives about the world we inhabit and reorders our priorities with regards to how we ought to live. Inevitably, this propels us to meaningful action and a radical life-style that mirror the intentions of God. Drawn closer and closer to the heart of God, we become more in tune with God's will and with single mindedness express our love through obedience.

The life of Thomas Merton is a testament to the power of a life lived in contemplative action. Merton's disciplined cultivation of his interior life shaped his intentional and vigorous engagement in the world. The fluid movement of contemplation and action that he exemplified toward the latter stages of his life came out of humble and often precarious beginnings.

The pages of *The Seven Storey Mountain*[2] and *The Secular Journal*[3] disclose an erudite, well traveled, and intensely reflective yet critical young Merton whose penetrating but sardonic commentaries seem to indicate ambivalent feelings toward the world he lived in. Yet buried underneath this love/hate relationship was a seed of contemplation that gradually grew and bore fruits, visibly in his social and political activism and invisibly in his deepening communion with God. Of his early writing, Merton notes:

> Certainly the views and aspirations expressed, at times, with such dogmatic severity, have come to be softened and tempered with the passage of time and with a more intimate contact with the spiritual problems of other people. I hope I may be forgiven for having allowed some of my youthful sarcasms to survive in these pages.[4]

Something drastic but deeply transformational must have occurred when he entered the cloistered walls of the Abbey of Gethsemane in Kentucky. What changed him from a distant and sarcastic spectator to a quiet yet radical, engaged, and socially conscious Trappist monk? In what way did the contemplative tradition of this monastic community inform and shape his views, attitudes, and responses to what was going on during his time? Had detachment from the world and attachment to God Alone removed the scales from his eyes and, in the process, enabled him to see the world and his place in it in a different light? His journals and other writings offer a window into this gradual and subtle transformation.

When he shut the world behind him and entered the disciplined life of contemplation, he stepped into the reality that mattered to him most—God Alone. The cares of the world were replaced with caring for one thing only, to be in the presence of God in silence and solitude. Henri Nouwen, reflecting on his encounter with Merton, observed that this new desert[5] transformed the monk into a fierce advocate of silence in the life of others. His commitment to provide spiritual direction for students in the abbey was his way of encountering them as they were, without their personas or masks, and honoring the solitude that lived within them.[6] He was able to see beyond mere appearances and touch the very heart of God within them. In this interior space, Merton experienced both the majesty and nearness of God and came to understand the contemplative life as:

> The deepening of faith and of the personal dimensions of liberty and apprehension to the point where our direct union with God is realized and experienced. We awaken not only to a realization of the immensity and majesty of God out there as King and Ruler of the universe (which He is) but also a more intimate and more wonderful perception of Him as directly and personally present in our own being.[7]

Consumed by the fire of divine love, he learned to be still yet fully awake to God's lure and invitation to greater intimacy. Even his depression and dark nights became an occasion to enter deeply into the heart of God. By welcoming his suffering as a guest that bears the gift of perseverance, character and hope, his life was transformed into the likeness of Jesus Christ: lavish and fearless in expressing love to others.

With this came the discovery of compassion, another fruit of an expanding life of interiority. The quiet yet transforming power of contemplation in his life brought him beyond the confines of the cloistered walls of the abbey and into a world that urgently needed a prophetic voice. Merton's experience through silence and solitude of the depth of God's love for all humanity redefined his monastic vocation as a social calling. The social and political unrest of the 1960s touched the core of his being and he felt compelled to confront it not on the streets but in the garden of his interior life.

> A certain depth of disciplined experience is a necessary ground for fruitful action. Without a more profound human understanding derived from exploration of the inner ground of human existence, love will tend to be superficial and deceptive. Traditionally, the ideas of prayer, meditation and contemplation have been associated with this deepening of one's personal life and this expansion of the capacity to understand and serve others.[8]

Merton links purposeful action with a heart that is fully awake, cognizant of its true condition, and transformed by the fiery love of God. Without a secure and rich inner ground and an experiential knowledge of the love of God for humanity, all labor is in vain.

CONTEMPLATIVE ACTION

The life of Thomas Merton is an embodiment of contemplative action. His commitment to social justice is deeply rooted in his remarkable devotion to God. With Merton as an example, we discover the importance of cultivating a life of interiority as we attempt to further social transformation both in our personal lives and in our therapeutic practice. Without the "depth of disciplined experience" and the "exploration of the inner ground," as Merton calls it, service to others becomes paternalistic, intrusive, and idolatrous. Conversely, when energized by divine love, the "capacity to understand and serve others" becomes a genuine expression of compassion and a strengthening of human solidarity.

Buddhist teacher Jack Kornfield echoes the same sentiment when he says that "true compassion . . . is never based on fear or pity but is a deep supportive response of the heart based on the dignity, integrity, and well-being of every single creature."[9] We stand side by side with those who are afflicted as a way of extending and making visible God's steadfast commitment to reach out to, embrace, and transform the suffering of a broken world.

Behind stories of depression, anxiety, relational rifts within marriages and families, substance abuse, domestic violence, and the like are social viruses, often undetected and all too menacing, that creep into the psyche of individuals and society. These include racism, sexism, classism, ageism, and the like. In counseling, the excessive focus on the individual as both the primary cause of suffering and the sole agent of change sometimes obscures the social dimension of illness formation and change. Conversely, the contemplative vision allows us to penetrate deeply into these realities and brings to our awareness the systemic nature of suffering and transformation.

By virtue of our shared humanity, the suffering of others reflects our own brokenness and propensity to hurt each other, while the healing of others is tied to our willingness to stand next to them in solidarity. This compassionate response is borne out of listening and looking deeply into each other's hearts where we discover the face of God who dwelt among us in Jesus Christ and who identified with and entered into our pain and suffering in order to transform it.

Regrettably, the seamless yet intricate connection between the personal and social worlds is usually truncated or severed in the training of Christian counselors. The emphasis still revolves around the care and healing of the singular self to the neglect of the wider social context in which the individual lives. Depression among women, for example, is partly but significantly caused by both covert and overt experiences of sexism at home, in the workplace, and in society at large. Yet, this societal virus might escape the attention of the clinician who narrowly focuses only on the personal or private dimension of depression.

Louise's haggard face reveals years of unhappiness and excruciating feelings of emptiness and unrequited love from her husband of eighteen years and two teenage children. She came to get some help for her depression, which manifests itself mostly in anger and irritability. One time she showed up visibly distraught, her body shaking and her face red with indignation. The ride to downtown was very "unpleasant . . . the train was packed and I could not breathe. There were just too many people and I just could not stand it," she complained. She was seething with anger as she reported this awful experience on the train.

As is customary, I encouraged Louise to express her anger without judging herself, as she usually does, for having such a strong and negative reaction. I reminded her to stay with the feeling, feeling it in her body, being aware of thoughts that accompany the feeling and memories that are triggered by it with curiosity and hospitality. It became more evident to Louise, as the session progressed, that this anger may have stemmed from her resentment toward being the sole caregiver in her family, always ensuring that everyone else's needs came first before her own.

"How did you learn this role?" I asked. Without flinching, Louise said, "From my own mother who spent most of her life caring for all of us. I learned it from her. But I am tired. I have nothing else to give."

Then she started to tear up and the anger that was so palpable at the beginning turned into an expression of deep sadness and hurt. We lingered there for a moment in silence, without words and without any attempt to explore or probe or intervene. I sat there deeply moved by the depth of her pain and suffering. I sat there also as a witness to the dawning of an increased level of self-awareness and acceptance.

That conversation signaled a crucial turn in Louise's view of herself as a woman and in her understanding of how her identity has been formed by both her personal and social worlds. Our subsequent therapeutic work involved a great deal of exploration in this area. Along with her expanding vision of herself came a new understanding of the bio-psycho-social and spiritual causes of depression and varied approaches to treatment. Her depression is no longer just a private matter. She is now starting to recognize the interplay between the personal and societal dimensions in both the formation and mitigation of her depression. Beliefs, practices, and attitudes about what it means to be a woman that she has internalized over the years are slowly surfacing and being given ongoing attention. The process of looking deeply into herself has led to a heightened sense of self-understanding and agency.

Any counselor adept in multi-cultural counseling would be able to help Louise discover aspects of her condition that she has not recognized before. For many counselors, addressing these issues is grounded in the conviction that "all behaviors are learned and displayed within cultural contexts,"[10] social structures, and worldviews. For a contemplative counselor, however, the dual focus on both the personal and social in counseling is more than just a matter of the interplay of personal and social dynamics. The contemplative counselor's focus also has a theological or religious dimension to it in that sustained interest and active engagement in both personal and social transformation emanates from deep within, from a heart transformed and nurtured by a life of contemplation.

Drawing motivation, strength, and direction from this inner, mindful, and quiet place is important on several fronts. First, by going inward in prayer, silence, and solitude, we retreat from all the noise, busyness, and chaos that hinder our ability to see things as they are; it is an unmasking of illusion, if you will. In this space of relative clarity and distance, we become aware of and can speak to the myriad issues that obstruct an integrated and mindful existence, both our own and that of others. The call to "act justly, and to love mercy, and to walk humbly with your God" (Mi 6:8) is no longer just a catchy phrase, but a call we seek to respond to both personally and professionally.

Merton sees this large-scale transformation as purely the work of God who is personally and deeply invested in redeeming the world, not from a distance, but by dwelling among us.

> The rebirth of [man] and of society on a transcultural level is a rebirth into the transformed and redeemed time, the time of the kingdom, the time of the Sprit. It means a disintegration of the social and cultural self, the product of merely human history, and the reintegration of that self in Christ, in salvation history, in the mystery of redemption, in the Pentecostal new creation.[11]

In counseling, this means exposing both the illusion of the centrality of the self and the insufficiency of an atomist view of the self. Merton, gleaning from the work of A. Reza Arasteh, a Persian psychologist with whom he had corresponded to learn more about Eastern traditions, observed that most psychotherapy tends to settle with merely "curing the neurosis by adaptation to society."[12] This skewed stance is legitimized in a culture that champions "cerebral, competitive, acquisitive forms of ego-affirmation,"[13] which then lead to "an apparently very active and productive mode of life, but in reality . . . stifles true growth, leaves people lost, alienated, frustrated and bored without any way of knowing what is wrong with them."[14] Had I just focused singly on the personal dimension of Louise's depression, working through her anger, teaching her assertiveness skills and self-care, encouraging a pro-active behavioral regimen, and so forth without assisting her in recognizing and addressing her depression's societal origins, the healing she was seeking might not have been possible. Her depressive symptoms may have been alleviated, but she may have remained out of sync with her deeper truth and out of touch with her core being.

The practice of contemplation intensifies the counselor's capacity for awareness of and critical engagement with what lies behind the veil of therapeutic culture. Contemplation encourages the counselor to seek new pathways for the perpetual "human task of maturation and self discovery."[15] Contemplative and mindfulness practices widen our gaze beyond the consulting room and support the counselor in looking deeply into the values and practices of our society that stifle interdependence and affirm acquisitive forms of ego-affirmations.

Mindfulness and contemplation enable the counselor to more readily admit his or her own participation in the endorsement of those values and practices. The interior journey confronts us with the reality that "the problem, the distorted belief, is not out there somewhere, but in here, in my own broken heart."[16] This self-reflection is often disconcerting and painfully revealing, yet through it we gain confidence in initiating and furthering the task of increasing personal and social maturity.

Sometimes though, it is easier to stay within the comforts of the therapeutic frame. Doing so, however, insulates and isolates the counselor from becoming personally involved and professionally responsible for addressing ingrained systemic realities that promote mindless conformity and obscure truth. In the clinical setting, this means taking a second and penetrating look at prevailing methods of counseling that are individualistic in orientation and then bringing to light the value system they privilege.

By looking deeply into our own profession, we will also discover the "lack of a theory of cultural oppression." This lack contributes to "the development of worldviews [that] continue to foster cultural blindness within the counseling profession."[17] The contemplative vision sees beyond the veneer of our profession and realizes the urgent need to commit oneself toward the radical transformation of the person *and* his or her social context. This is integral to our vocation as Christian practitioners called and sent by God "to increase the love of self, God, and neighbor, and to promote a just social order and a livable environment."[18] In unique ways and through the grace of God, counseling becomes a way ushering in the reign of God here on earth through the counselor's active participation in the restoration and healing of broken selves and the broken world we inhabit.

In my work with Louise, this has taken the form of maintaining a dual focus on her personal lived experience of depression and the larger social and cultural context she finds herself in. There have been occasions when the societal dimension of her personal complaint of depression was magnified and explored more deliberately. Louise gradually became more aware that the beliefs and attitudes about women that she internalized growing up—such as a woman's identity is primarily that of nurturer and caregiver, self-sacrificing and self-giving at all times for the welfare of her family—have limited both her self-concept and her options for personal growth and development. She has resented the fact that she was pigeonholed into this role and she has felt trapped, immobilized, and lost. She held all the pain, anger, hurt, disappointment, bitterness, and helplessness in her heart for years and, as a consequence, these feelings finally evolved into a full-blown depression. She felt even more disillusioned when she realized through our joint exploration that the role that was stifling her had been sanctioned and normalized by the larger culture. "I don't know who I am or what I am!" she cried out in anguish and desperation.

Witnessing Louise peel away the layers of unprocessed pain and suffering buried in her heart for so long was difficult. Yet, it was necessary because healing comes not by moving away from pain, but moving toward and through it with courage and perseverance.

By going inward, we discover a new depth of solidarity with the rest of humanity. Contrary to popular belief, contemplation, though deeply personal, is not a private matter; in solitude we find the basis of true community. Merton experienced this in the seclusion of his hermitage. He discovered, after many years in solitude, that what is most personal is also universal, that at the very core of his being he shares the same human condition as everyone else. With a tinge of repentance, he declares:

> And now I owe everyone else in the word a share in that life. My first duty is to start, for the first time, to live as a member of a human race, which is no more (and no less) ridiculous than I am myself. And my first human act is the recognition of how much I owe everybody else.[19]

Merton's conviction came out of the painful and disturbing realization that "Auschwitz, Hiroshima, Vietnam, and Watts were present in the intimate core of his own being . . . that in him lived humankind, in all its misery but also in its longing for love."[20]

In the company of no one but God Alone, Merton's heart broke open and there he saw that the image of every man and woman resided within him. This self-understanding fueled his commitment to use his pen as a weapon against violence to human bodies, minds, and souls. It was faith in the God disclosed by Christ that inspired Merton to social and political action.

> I am against war, against violence, against revolution, for peaceful settlement of differences, for nonviolent but nevertheless radical changes. Change is needed, and violence will not really change anything: at most it will only transfer power from one set of bullheaded authorities to another. If I say these things, it is not because I am more interested in politics than in the Gospel. I am not. But today more than ever the Gospel commitment has political implications, because you cannot claim to be "for Christ" and espouse a political cause that implies callous indifference to the needs of the millions of human beings and even cooperate in their destruction.[21]

The social ills that we encounter today are no different from the ones Merton had to confront during his time. There is still racial strife; women and defenseless children are still being subjected to abuse of all sorts; the gap between the rich and the poor grows wider; discrimination based on gender, sexual orientation, class, age, and religion still abounds. As counselors in the contemplative tradition, active engagement in the promotion of a just social order must be motivated by compassion toward those victimized by the structures of domination and the abuse of power, in other words, compassion grounded in the compassion of God.

Pursuing social justice in the realm of our personal lives can be daunting and draining at times, especially when life is already riddled with so many other commitments and professional challenges. When it comes to the struggle for social justice, some have opted out because of its demands; others have been pushed aside because of their radical ideas; still others have become inactive, or worse, disillusioned by the absence of positive outcomes or reinforcements. It is, after all, easy to just turn our backs from the harsh realities of this world and confine ourselves to our personally constructed fortress. Choosing apathy over active participation in ushering in the reign of God in this broken world, however, is a sign of unbelief and a denial of human dignity.

In clinical settings, horrific stories of rape, childhood sexual abuse, domestic violence, disintegration of the marital and family unit due to infidelity, substance abuse and dependence, addictions, and the like often evoke a sense of despair and powerlessness over against the reality and consequences of human depravity. Often, the task of raising a client's consciousness with respect to the fact that our "personal identities and our social fabric are fundamentally ordered by a variety of oppressive social systems"[22] is obstructed by the client's own reticence and the pressure to provide short-term work with visible results. The enormity of this task often renders counselors overwhelmed, feeling alone and sometimes unsupported.

The regular rhythm of silence and solitude of the heart not only acts as a buffer against all this; it also serves as a reminder that this burden is not ours to carry alone. When we gaze upon the face of God we are invited to lay down our burdens, disappointments, fears, and all the challenges that assail our justice and peacemaking efforts. The liberating power of God's love that conquered death by coming face to face with suffering also empowers us to rise up and come alongside those who are wounded, broken, and despairing. With the love of God as the motive power, we are reenergized to continue the struggle for love and justice by seeking "mutuality and reciprocity rather than dominance and subordination in social relationships."[23]

COMPASSION RWANDA

As said previously, the contemplative spirit sharpens the ears of our hearts so that we can hear the still, small, and gentle voice of God (Ps 46:10). Hearing God's voice in silence and solitude leads to the freedom needed "to act justly and to love mercy and to walk humbly with God" (Mi 6:8). Indeed, the closer we move toward the heart of God the more we share God's passion for justice and peace, which, for the contemplative counselor, means becoming fully engaged in social activism, advocacy, solidarity, and compassion for and faithful accompaniment with those who suffer from the life-negating domination systems of our world.

Along with several colleagues, I came to understand more deeply the nature of engagement in the struggle for social justice and healing during a recent mission to Rwanda. We went to Rwanda to provide therapeutic support for the survivors of the 1994 genocide.

Our experience in Rwanda came about because our hearts had been readied through contemplation to hear and answer the call to show compassion toward those who are still struggling with the residual and persistent effects of trauma experienced during the genocide. The experience was life-transforming, emerging as it did from a mindful and contemplative awareness of our personal and societal responsibility to pursue justice and peace wherever we are.

The divine invitation to participate in efforts to bring about justice and peace is on-going. The daily rhythms of prayer, *lectio divina*, silence, and solitude had predisposed us to respond to this invitation with the confidence that we were following Jesus in the way of God. These habits of the soul calmed our worries and fears and deepened our compassion and empathy for those who are still suffering from the trauma of genocide. Indeed, we discovered that our spiritual poverty was continually met with the overflowing grace and provision of God during that journey with our Rwandan brothers and sisters.

The reality of our spiritual poverty became evident as soon as we stepped onto the red soil of Rwanda, the land of a thousand hills. Rwanda is a country traumatized by a horrific past, and yet its people have managed to rise from the ashes with resilience and courage. The genocide of 1994 is estimated to have claimed the lives of over a million innocent and defenseless people in a hundred days. The genocide was carefully planned and systemically carried out. The architects of genocide convinced the core of the Hutu population that every Tutsi, young and old, male and female, must be purged from their midst. These were their neighbors, friends, schoolmates, fellow workers, relatives, and close associates who, during those dark days, became the targets of hate and unspeakable violence.

Fifteen years had passed and the country had taken radical steps to deal with the racial strife that fueled the genocide by creating a culture and a country of one people, the "Rwandese." The old social, economic, and political lines of demarcation gradually dissolved as the Rwandese began rebuilding their nation. This process has been challenging and inspiring, although finding the delicate balance between bringing the perpetrators of genocide to justice and promoting reconciliation remains a focal point of healing.

The journey has been painstakingly long and arduous. Even in the midst of profound changes and development, the long-term effects of trauma continue to haunt the people. Vast number of individuals witnessed multiple atrocities, including the heinous deaths of close family members, rape, mutilation, and other traumatic experiences. Due to the number of survivors of the genocide and the scarcity of available resources, sustaining physical, emotional, and psychological support for these victims has been a formidable challenge.

The task before us felt insurmountable, yet being anchored and rooted in God's love for the afflicted kept us centered, fully dependent on God, and available to the Rwandese we worked with. Our contemplative practice led us to the experience that Merton described—a profound sense of human community and solidarity grounded in the unconditional love of God.

There were about a hundred Rwandese who came every day to learn more about trauma in the hope that they might discover a pathway to healing. They shared with us their on-going battle with the residual and often debilitating effects of their traumatic experiences. They talked about their attempts to recover. Underneath those faces that carried unfathomable anguish, behind those tears of excruciating pain, sadness, and anger, and hidden in stories of horror, guilt, and confusion was a spirit of resilience and hope. Though their lives bore witness to the terror of genocide, their souls whispered: "We are hard pressed on every side, but not crushed; perplexed, but not in despair; persecuted, but not abandoned; struck down, but not destroyed" (2 Cor 4:8-9).

There was no other way to reach out to our Rwandese friends than to be received by them first, and to honor them by accepting a hospitality that was borne out of suffering and recovery. Their hospitality disarmed our feelings of inadequacy, fears, and anxieties, and their joyful embrace included their acceptance of our gift of presence, knowledge, and skill. Our intention to come alongside them was met with simple and unreserved gestures of warm reception punctuated with the words: "Welcome. You are welcome here."

The contemplative practice of looking deeply allowed us to recognize clearly God's abiding presence during our time in Rwanda. Whether we were energized by the enthusiastic crowd or overwhelmed by their unmet needs; inspired by stories of resistance against despair and hopelessness or stirred deeply by the outpouring of grief; sustained by a simple act of sacrifice or stricken by illness, God's presence remained the same, always quiet, reassuring, overflowing.

Anchored by our sense of God's presence, we approached our work of teaching and counseling with quiet confidence not in ourselves but in God who had began a good work in us (Phil 1:6) and whose grace was sufficient (2 Cor 12:9) during times of weakness, self-doubt, and seemingly insurmountable challenges. Our spiritual poverty awakened us to an experience of fullness and gratitude when we witnessed the transformation of lives as a result of our work and God's healing power.

One individual who came to us for help commented on how simple and yet profoundly reassuring mindful breathing was for her, especially when done with the Jesus Prayer. She had not realized that breathing in the words "Lord, Jesus Christ" and breathing out the words "have mercy on me" could bring so much peace and hope, especially when painful memories surfaced. This simple yet profound prayer became a source of peace, hope, healing, and deepening faith in the God who is as intimately connected to her as the air she breathes.

The stories of the Rwandese people with whom we lived and worked are now forever linked to our own narratives; their humanity reflects our shared identity in Christ; their growing transformation and liberation speak of our commitment to be in solidarity with them in their suffering. We went to Rwanda to give something of ourselves and we left deeply enriched by the gift we received, of unwavering faith in God at all times and in all ways.

BREAD FOR THE JOURNEY

In Thomas Merton, we discover that communion with God in prayer, silence, and solitude inevitably leads to communion with others in solidarity with the rest of humanity. Merton's writings have become a source of great inspiration and have encouraged me to connect the adoration of God with a commitment to stand in solidarity with the oppressed and to accompany those who suffer under the structures of domination and violence that plague our world.

In Rwanda, we discovered the human soul in its darkest as well as its finest hour. This cross-cultural experience has made us acutely aware that, despite the geographical divide, our humanity is one by virtue of our shared identity in Christ.

As contemplative counselors, our task is not only caring for the wounded and singular self. Looking deeply into the heart of our clients, we see both the traumas and tragedies of human life together and the face of God who is intently involved in the restoration of human community.

Personally, we participate in God's ongoing efforts to unmask the principalities and powers, which try to destroy the divine image and dignity of all human beings, through our social activism, advocacy, and faithful accompaniment of those who are oppressed, exploited, and violated. The motivation for participating in the struggle against injustice of any kind, of course, is not mere altruism. It is far more basic than that. The suffering of every individual, whether self-imposed or inflicted by others, reflects the problem of estrangement that we all struggle with. All healing is connected because we are all deeply connected to each other by virtue of our relation to the ground of our being. In the healing of others is our own healing; in the liberation of others is our own liberation; in the redemption of others is our own redemption.

The contemplative movement of descending inward to be with God Alone and ascending outward to be with God's people undergirds our commitment to both personal and social transformation, to our work with individual clients and to our participation in the larger struggle against all that diminishes, damages, or destroys life.

Chapter 6

❧ CHRISTIAN CONTEMPLATION: A WAY OF WORSHIP

Just as one who looks at the sun cannot but fill the eyes with light,
so the one who gazes intently into the heart cannot fail to be illuminated.

St. Hesychios the Priest

The journey of the contemplative counselor is marked and nour-ished by the ongoing cultivation of our interior garden through specific habits of the soul. The contemplative practices of the prayer of silence, *lectio divina*, prayer with icons, and loving-kindness medi-tation are explored more fully in this chapter with the intention of providing concrete directions for those who desire to pursue a life of contemplation.

Suffice it to say at this point that choosing the path of contempla-tion is a way of responding to God's on-going invitation for commu-nion and union moment by moment in our lives. Cultivation of the seed of contemplation that is planted in the interior garden of our soul uproots the weeds of self-assertion and self-possession and bears the fruit of surrender and an experiential and loving knowledge of God. In the descent inward, we become acutely aware of God's unconditional and diffusive love that calls us out into the world so that others may share in it as well.

Within the context of our chosen vocation, contemplative awareness yields to an integrative, mindful, compassionate attitude toward our clients who are struggling with the existential problem of estrangement. We approach the task of counseling with a focused yet quiet attention, embodying the attitudes of curiosity, receptivity, openness, stillness, and surrender (CROSS)[1] to what is unfolding in the present moment. Such a therapeutic stance is fashioned by the contemplative vision of clients as honored guests; by the conviction that the suffering they carry can be redemptive, a gateway to a transformed and mindful life; and by the belief that in and with God, healing and the transformation of brokenness into wholeness is made possible.

The contemplative life also expands our horizon to include an unwavering commitment to manifest the reign of God in the personal, professional, and social domains of our lives. As counselors, we have been given access to people whose inner worlds are reflections of a broken outer world. The heightened empathy and compassion that emerges from a contemplative encounter with God leads us to stand alongside victims and survivors of both individual and systemic forces of evil by actively engaging in the pursuit of both individual and social transformation.

The contemplative life demands a radical commitment to God Alone. In the experience of communion with God, we begin to reorder our lives in the concreteness of our own unique context in a manner that reflects God's own character and intention. Simply put, the path of contemplation collapses into and emerges out of a life of worship marked by a profound longing to "dwell in the house of the Lord . . . to gaze upon the beauty of the Lord, and to seek him in his temple" (Ps 27:4).

There are habits of the soul that help sustain our commitment to a life of contemplation, specific spiritual practices that will promote the ongoing formation of the contemplative counselor. The list that follows is not at all exhaustive. It is meant merely as a guidepost as we continue on the path toward ever-deepening intimacy with God. Tending our interior ground can take many different forms, all of which yield to a common experience of being transformed into the likeness of the Christ.

SOLITUDE

The earthly ministry of Jesus was punctuated and supported by his regular solitary fellowship with God (Mk 1:35, et al.). It was intrinsic to the rhythm of his life and afforded him with the opportunity to rest his whole being in God, to commune with God and to school himself in the will of God for him. In other words, solitude is deeply relational, a time alone with God that sharpens the "quality of our awareness of our relationship with all that lies within and which gives meaning and purpose."[2] We descend interiorly and with wakefulness, attentiveness, and intentionality enter into the presence of God.

The felt need that many experience to retreat from the world, either literally or metaphorically, to be with God Alone, witnesses to the awakening of the transforming desire to be in an intimate relationship with God. Because we are created in the image of God, we long to be in communion with God who "calls us to a relationship with himself that makes us to be sharers in the eternal, perfect solitude of Christ the Word."[3] Solitude transcends space and time when conceived of ultimately as solitude of the heart.

There are times, of course, when solitude evokes feelings of aloneness and loneliness. In fact, being alone can expose our existential dilemma of vulnerability and isolation. Yet, part of the spiritual life is to welcome such feelings with hospitality and to endure them with patience and courage. It is precisely the recognition and acceptance of our fundamental aloneness that gives way to an openness to God's promise of faithful accompaniment. St. John of the Cross says, "Start from where you are. Be yourself. Pray in the way that it is given to you to pray by letting your prayer flow from the reality of your life."[4]

LECTIO DIVINA

The spiritual practice of divine reading, or *lectio divina*, is a way of contemplative listening to and praying with the Scriptures. Quite different from speed reading, *lectio divina* is a way of inclining the ears of the heart to listen to the word of the God with both attention and a willingness "to be read by it." In *lectio divina*, the contemplative anticipates a deep encounter with God who comes to us in the words of Scripture. This ancient practice has four movements: (1) *lectio* or reading/listening to God through the Scriptures; (2) *meditatio* or meditating upon the text, letting it speak to us freely and wholly until it becomes part of us; (3) *oratio* or verbal prayer in which we are in loving conversation with God who "spoke the word" to us for our nourishment and transformation; and (4) *contemplatio* or contemplation where we rest in silence before God, simply *being with* God in peace and adoration. Here is my summary of this practice:

Spiritual Habit of the Soul I: Personal Lectio Divina

Choose a particular text of the Scriptures that you wish to pray. Any passage in the book of Psalms would be a good place to start. The intent is to predispose yourself to hear the voice of God in the Word of God.

Place yourself in a comfortable position and allow yourself to become silent. Become mindful of your breathing. Observe each breath in and each breath out, remembering that breath is the gift of God, the gift of life itself. Just be aware of your breathing until your body is relaxed, your mind quiet, and your heart at rest before the Lord.

Turn to the chosen text and read it slowly and gently. Try to savor each word or phrase, let it rest in your heart. As the passage settles within, be mindful of the still, small voice of God inviting you to enter deeply into his presence.

Take a word or phrase or sentence that caught your attention. Ponder it, memorize it, and slowly repeat it to yourself, perhaps in sync with your breathing. Allow it to speak to your inner world, be open to its direction, receive it with hospitality, and converse with it.

Speak to God, either in words or images. Simply dialogue with God. Dialogue implies mutuality so listen as well as speak. You may take the promptings of your conscience as you meditate on Scripture to be one of the many ways God speaks to you. Talk with God about what you have heard or discovered during your meditation.

Finally, simply rest in God's embrace. Use words or images when they are helpful to foster intimacy or let go of them when they are no longer necessary. Rejoice in your experiential knowledge that God is both within and around you, in words and in silence.

End your time of fellowship with God by praying the *Gloria Patri*—slowly, gently and attentive to its every word. *Glory be to the Father, and to Son, and to the Holy Spirit. As it was in the beginning, is now, and ever shall be, world without end. Amen.*

THE PRAYER OF SILENCE

Prayer is not something that we do; it is who we are. Whatever form prayer takes, at its most fundamental level it expresses our true nature as people who have been created and who are being sustained and loved deeply by our Creator. Prayer is grounded in the reality that we are bound to and wholly dependent on God Alone. The moment we raise our eyes or bow our heads or utter words or simply remain in stillness we consent to God's invitation to enter into his presence fully awake and aware that "in him we move and live and have our being" (Acts 17:28).

The invitation to communion and union with God, which, generally speaking, is what contemplation is about, is a universal calling. The invitation to move toward the heart of God is made available to all, without limits, restrictions, or conditions. Contemplative prayer, however, "is a particular expression of our universal call to faith, hope, and love."[5] It is a "prayer of silence, simplicity, contemplative and meditative unity, a deep personal integration in an attentive, watchful listening of the heart. The response such prayer calls forth is not usually one of jubilation or audible witness; it is a wordless and total surrender of the heart in silence."[6]

The soul habit of contemplative prayer involves our willingness to shut off the noise of this world and the chatter of our minds so that we can descend interiorly into our heart fully awake and attentive to the still, small voice of God (Ps 46:10). This "watchful listening of the heart" is a way of gazing "upon the beauty of the Lord" (Ps 27:4). It leads to the renewal and nourishment of body, mind, and spirit. Through contemplative prayer we enter into the presence of God with openness, receptivity, and simplicity of the heart, an experience that is marked by self-emptying and surrender.

The practice of quieting our mind and listening helps to foster interior silence. It is something that anyone can do, either alone in the privacy of one's space or in the midst of a crowd. For beginners, it is extremely helpful to find a relatively quiet space to practice this listening exercise for at least ten minutes a day either in the morning or at night. With practice, the capacity to enter into interior silence at any moment during the day and at any place grows. The blossoming of this spiritual habit of the soul is cultivated by perseverance and patience and graced by the on-going, transforming work of the Holy Spirit within us.

Spiritual Habit of the Soul II: Listening Exercise

Sit in a comfortable chair in a quiet space. Place your hands on your lap with your palms facing up. Close your eyes and take a few deep breaths. Become mindful of the air that is coming into and going out of your body.

Notice the sounds you hear about you. Listen first for the fainter, more distant sounds, then those that are nearby. Simply become aware of them. Continue to breathe mindfully.

Now turn your attention to your heart. Pay attention to the sound of your heartbeat, while you continue to breathe mindfully.

Notice the deepening sound of silence in this place of prayer. Listen to the words of the Lord: "Be still and know that I am God."

A variation of the listening exercise is the Jesus Prayer, done in concert with your breathing. Again, the intent is to become mindful of the presence of God within and around us. As the prayer leads us inward, we consent to God's invitation to communion and intimate fellowship. My summary:

Spiritual Habit of the Soul III: The Jesus Prayer

Take a comfortable posture and close your eyes. Spend some time in quieting yourself. Become aware of the presence of God within and around you

Be mindful of your breathing for a while. Remembering that breath is the gift of God, become aware of the air as you breathe in and breathe out. Linger here for a moment.

Think of breathing as your way of reaching out to God. Let it remind you that you are deeply connected to the One, who is the source of life.

As you breathe in, say the first part of the prayer, *Lord Jesus Christ.* As you do so, imagine that you are breathing into yourself the love, grace, and presence of the Lord Jesus. Linger here for a moment.

As you breathe out, say the second part of the prayer, *have mercy on me*. Imagine you are breathing out of yourself all your cares and worries, anything and everything that gets in the way of your openness to God's mercy and grace. Linger here for a moment.

Breathe in the words, *Lord Jesus Christ*; breathe out the words, *have mercy on me*.

When you are ready to come out of the silence, open your eyes.

Practice the Jesus Prayer at other times of the day, for example, when riding the bus, doing the dishes, taking a walk, or working in the garden.

The open and receptive posture we develop in our devotional life transfers quite seamlessly into our therapeutic work. With our mind already quieted and our heart and soul surrendered to God, we approach the therapeutic space poised to listen deeply to the cries of those whom we counsel. Such a welcoming stance inspires our clients to come as they are and to lay down their burdens without feeling judged or rushed. It enables them to experience being held, accompanied and understood as they journey toward healing and transformation.

PRAYING WITH ICONS

The loving gaze of the soul on God in contemplation is a profound act of worship. The Psalmist says: "One thing I ask of the Lord, this is what I seek; that I may dwell in the house of the LORD, all the days of my life, to gaze upon the beauty of the LORD and to seek him in his temple" (Ps 27:4). The psalmist's only desire, in the midst of threats and attacks from his oppressors, is to dwell in the temple, beholding the beauty and the glory of the Lord. In gazing upon the Lord, courage, confidence, and undivided attention displace fear and estrangement.

One of the ways of cultivating worshipful attention to God is praying with icons. The use of icons to deepen one's prayer life is quite common among Christians, particularly those of the Eastern Orthodox tradition. For centuries icons were the dominant form of religious art in the Orthodox tradition and are still afforded liturgical significance in the life of faith.

The visual representation of a religious reality fosters a sense of stillness and undivided attention for the contemplative beholder. The two-dimensional sacred art inspires us to be still, to behold, to gaze upon, to pray, to be fully present with and attentive to what is represented before us. With our eyes fixed on the icon, in quiet and prayerful anticipation, we see beyond the image and penetrate the depths of what it symbolizes. The icon becomes another portal, a gateway into "persons and events seen in the light of the transfiguring and redeeming grace of God; they take us up into the light of God's eternity, grace, and truth, and nourish in us the Life in His Name which is manifested through the Incarnation."[7] To put it another way, icons are created with the sole purpose of disclosing a divine reality that beckons our attention and ushers us into another place, right into the depths of our being, to meet with God.

The role of icons in deepening a life lived in contemplation became more evident to me during my stay at a monastery. I spent every morning looking at an ancient Byzantine icon called "The Holy Trinity" created by a monk named Andrei Rublev in 1425. The icon is a representation of an event recorded in Genesis 18 known as the "hospitality of Abraham." However, it omits the characters of Abraham, Sarah, and the servants in order to focus our attention solely on the images of three angels seated at table, which take us into the mysterious relationships within the Trinity between the Father, the Son, and the Holy Spirit.

The moment I laid eyes on the icon I was drawn by what seemed an open invitation to join the intimate gathering of fellowship and communion they shared. Alone and lonely on this spiritual pilgrimage, part of me wanted to run quickly to find consolation in the figures seated at table. But another part of me wanted to run away for fear that I did not deserve to be there in the first place. Either way, I was stricken by my tendency to ignore or brush aside these conflicting and unpleasant feelings. I was not being mindful or hospitable to all the emotions that the icon evoked within me. Instead, I experienced a strong impulse to avoid and deny the pain of aloneness and loneliness either by running toward the table or by running away from the table in the icon.

"The Trinity" by Andrei Rublev
The Tretyakov Gallery, Moscow, Russia

Yet the Christ-figure seated in the center of the icon seemed to invite me to come just as I was, with all my conflicted feelings and my deep longings for companionship. The hand that gestured me to come was the same hand that had been pierced with nails on the cross, opening the way to this place of communion. So I focused my gaze on Christ, "the image of the invisible God" (Col 1:15), as I slowly approached the table fellowship. The transcendent, infinite God is an immanent, welcoming God in the person of Jesus Christ who endured persecution, loneliness, and abandonment, and offered his life so that we might be transformed into the same image or likeness of God.

My prayerful gaze upon the icon brought me to a new experience of God's invitation to intimacy, one that profoundly awakened both my mind and my heart. As I drew near the table of the Lord, I felt encouraged to come as naked and vulnerable as possible, shedding off piece by piece every garment of self-assertion, pride, and unbelief and putting on the robe of self-denial, humility, and trust. As much as I felt exposed in the presence of God, I also sensed that I was being known intimately and loved wholeheartedly. This divine hospitality gave me the freedom to just sit at the table in silence and at peace with being there just as I am, in communion with the Triune God.

While praying with the icon, I moved my gaze to the image on the right, which symbolizes the Holy Spirit. The green robe that is draped around this angel and the raised hand and head that are tilted to the right seem to indicate an unbroken unity between the Holy Spirit and the Son of God in fulfilling the will of the Father. Our entrance into this circle and ever-expanding communion of love is made possible through the external work of Jesus Christ and the internal work of the Holy Spirit within us.

As I looked at the image of the Holy Spirit, my consciousness was flooded with unpleasant feelings of self-determination and self-agency, feelings that are ever present in my life. I felt perturbed, guilty, and even ashamed of these feelings but in the hospitality of that moment I met them with openness. I remained transfixed on the angel's raised hand pointing toward the chalice as if bidding me to surrender all. It became apparent to me that I was being invited to be mindful and lay bare my soul, with all its grief, impurities, and wounds, before God for cleansing, forgiveness, and renewal. I stood there graced by the abiding presence of the Holy Spirit who once again welcomed me unreservedly to the table for nourishment and healing.

The tension between self-assertion and self-denial is difficult to resolve. It takes the guidance of the Spirit to realize the futility of willfulness and the economy of the willingness to submit.[8] Indeed, when it comes to the spiritual life, the action of the Holy Spirit both reflects and transcends the intention of the believer, and together the action of the Spirit and the intention of the believer yield the fruit of transformation.

The hospitality of the Son and of the Holy Spirit depicted in the icon evoked feelings of majesty, reverence, and awe as I gazed upon the angel who represents God the Father. Like the two angels whose heads are bowed in honor of the First Person of the Trinity, I also prostrated myself in my heart as an act of adoration and devotion to the One, whose self-revelation is an act of pure love.

Out of love, God created all there is and with love humankind came to be, bearing God's image and likeness. Despite humanity's attempts at self-possession, God remains faithful and steadfast in love—the central truth of the incarnation. Who can resist such a love? Who can exist apart from this love? Such were the thoughts and feelings that emerged from my contemplation of the icon.

As I looked upon the icon, I caught a glimpse of the beauty and unbroken union of the Godhead, a union that extends into all of creation. Gazing at Jesus meant being drawn into the depths of the Father's great love. Within the icon, the movement of the Son and the Spirit toward the Father and the movement of the Father to the Son is "a movement in which the one who prays is lifted up and held secure."[9] The experience of inclusion and divine embrace serves as an anchor as we move back into a world that is broken by exclusion and estrangement. The space at the middle is reserved for us, and yet it is not supposed to be filled permanently.

The descent inward into communion with God inevitably leads to an ascent outward to be in communion with the people of God. So we live, "knowing the Trinity is . . . involved in this circling movement: drawn by the Son toward the Father, drawn into the Father's breathing out of the Spirit so that the Son's life may be made real in the world. This is where contemplation and action become inseparable."[10]

My contemplation of Rublev's icon of "The Holy Trinity" deepened my conviction that it is the contemplative experience of union with God and others that grounds our personal and professional lives, and that moves us to seek the transformation and healing of both individuals and the social world that wounds those individuals. That is to say, through the balance of contemplation and action, Christ's life is made real in the world through the love and compassion of those who follow him.

PRAYER FOR UNITY

As Jesus' ministry on earth drew to a close, he prayed for unity among those whom the Father had given him (Jn 17:11, 21). Jesus formed a new community out of disparate and diverse individuals and this "united community and its unifying mission are meant to bear witness to the unique communication the Father has made to the world in sending his only Son."[11] The divine life is a life of communion and union, and participating in that life yields fruits of communion and union with others.

In Rublev's icon, we witness the overflowing union of the Triune God, spilling over, touching our broken selves, reframing our fragmented stories, and reconciling us to others so that our life in the world becomes a clear embodiment of God's love in the world. Unity is born out of love and, where there is love and unity, God is glorified and the community of love expands and encircles others into its fold.

Simply put, the prayer of Jesus for unity is the motivating force for his followers' "mission to awaken the world to the gifts that they have received, but which are destined for all. Both the sending of the Son and the Son's sending of the disciples into the world are the outcome of the Father's unreserved love—for Jesus, for the disciples, and for the world itself."[12]

For those of us engaged in caring for the souls of others, our ministry of inclusion and hospitality is an embodying of Christ in the world. And for the contemplative counselor who knows to "look deeply," the client is a living icon of Christ (Mt 25:40). When we sit with individuals in counseling, we see this image distorted, but never destroyed. Our contemplative stance allows us to see the beauty that is hidden behind the image that is deformed by the absence of love. Out of the experience of communion with the Triune God, we open the spaces of our hearts so that those who are hurting might feel included, accepted, and loved as they are.

The experience of feeling felt, seen, and heard by another, without judgment and conditions, breaks down the wall of isolation that suffering often brings and renders the client open to receive and give love. The image that has been distorted by the absence of love is slowly restored as clients experience a contemplative and mindful attitude of inclusion and hospitality. It is in this manner that we fulfill our iconic vocation, by pointing others to the only source of true, unconditional, and transforming love.

Indeed, both counselor and client are icons of God: born out of God's creative act and diffusive love and made in God's image and likeness (Gen 1:26-31). We came into being out of the intimate union and overflowing love of the Triune God. We are made out of love and for love and our life's purpose is to reflect and point others to this loving God. "Where love is missing all the elements of the imagery are deformed."[13]

The practice of loving-kindness meditation brings to mind God's compassion toward us, a compassion that entered into our own suffering through the incarnation of Jesus Christ. Such divine accompaniment in the midst of our pain and suffering enables us to approach our own wounds and those of our clients with an attitude of hospitality and non-judgmental acceptance. The experience of God's solidarity with us compels us to come alongside those who are stricken by a broken world with a compassionate heart. My summary:

Spiritual Habit of the Soul IV: Loving-Kindness Meditation

Sit quietly and take a few deep, mindful breaths. When a thought or feeling surfaces, just simply notice it, and then bring your attention back to your breathing

When you feel settled and at peace, acknowledge, without judging, any suffering or struggle you are aware of. Now bring to mind a person in your life who loves you very much, who delights in you and makes you feel good no matter what.

Imagine this person sitting in front of you or beside you at this very moment, extending his or her love and unconditional acceptance once again. Feel the other person's love coming toward you like warm rays of sunlight permeating your entire being, filling and warming your heart.

If you feel like your heart has been hardened by anger, sadness, pain, and suffering, fear not and don't lose heart. Instead let the love that is flowing from this person touch your heart, warming and nourishing it, making it alive once more.

As this healing love comes into you, feel your heart softening and overflowing with love and gratitude. Feel peaceful, whole, and replenished with love. Naturally, your love and gratitude begins to spill over, touching those around you and those whom you will meet today.

We all have within us the seed of contemplation. It has been planted in the interior garden of our soul by the God in whose image we are made and who longs for communion with us. The cultivation of our interior garden is both the work of the Holy Spirit within us and our own willingness to intentionally and mindfully practice contemplation. The seamless and cyclical movement of descending interiorly to be with God Alone and ascending exteriorly to be with the people of God marks the contours of contemplation. The contemplative vision is a gift received from God to be shared with both our clients and the world God loves.

> One thing I ask of the LORD
>> this is what I seek:
>> that I may dwell in the house of the LORD
>> all the days of my life,
>> to gaze upon the beauty of the LORD
>> and to seek him in his temple. Psalm 27:4

Soli Deo Gloria.

Notes

INTRODUCTION

1. See, for example, Jamie D. Aten and Mark M. Leach, *Spirituality and Therapeutic Process: A Comprehensive Resource from Intake to Termination* (Washington, D.C.: APA Books, 2008); Thomas G. Plante, *Spiritual Practices in Psychotherapy: Thirteen Tools for Enhancing Psychological Health* (Washington, D.C.: APA Books, 2009); P. Scott Richards and Allen E. Bergin, *A Spiritual Strategy for Counseling and Psychotherapy,* 2nd ed. (Washington, D.C.: APA Books, 2005); Len Sperry and Edward P. Schafranske, *Spiritually Oriented Psychotherapy* (Washington, D.C.: APA Books, 2004).

2. Gerald Corey, *Theory and Practice of Counseling and Psychotherapy* (Toronto: Thomson Brooks/Cole, 2008), 448ff.

3. Paul C. Vitz, *Psychology as Religion: The Cult of Self-Worship,* 2nd ed. (Grand Rapids: Eerdmans, 1977), 32.

4. All names in case vignettes have been changed to protect identities

5. Edward Teyber, *Interpersonal Process in Therapy: An Integrative Model,* 5th ed. (Toronto: Thomson Brooks/Cole, 2005), 20.

6. M. Basil Pennington, Thomas Keating and Thomas Clarke, *Finding Grace at the Center: The Beginning of Centering Prayer,* 3rd ed. (Woodstock Vt.: SkyLight Paths, 2007), 71.

7. Richard Rohr, *The Naked Now: Learning to See as the Mystics See* (New York: Crossroad, 2009).

8. Mary Jo Meadow, *Christian Insight Meditation: Following in the Footsteps of John of the Cross* (Boston: Wisdom Publications, 2007), 165.

CHAPTER 1: THE IDENTITY OF THE CONTEMPLATIVE COUNSELOR

1. Mark A. Hubble, Barry L. Duncan, and Scott D. Miller, *The Heart and Soul of Change: What Works in Therapy* (Washington: American Psychological Association, 2003), 1-22.

2. Ibid., 145.

3. Thomas Skovholt and Michael Ronnestad, *The Evolving Professional Self: Stages and Themes in Therapist and Counselor Development* (New York: Wiley, 1992), 11.

4. Ray S. Anderson, *Christians Who Counsel* (Grand Rapids: Zondervan, 1990), 162.

5. Ibid., 162.

6. Carl Goldberg, *On Being a Psychotherapist* (Northvale, N.J.: Jason Aronson, 1997), 49.

7. Ibid., 4.

8. Ibid., 5.

9. C.J. Groesbeck and B. Taylor, "The Psychiatrist as Wounded Physician," *American Journal of Psychoanalysis*, 37 (1971), 131–139

10. Goldberg, *On Being a Psychotherapist*, 13.

11. Ibid., 5.

12. Goldberg, *On Being a Psychotherapist*, 5.

13. Mark McMinn, *Psychology, Theology, and Spirituality in Christian Counseling* (Carol Stream, Ill.: Tyndale, 1996), 14.

14. Timothy Clinton and George Ohlschlager, *Competent Christian Counseling*, Vol. 1 (Colorado Springs: Waterbrook, 2002), 131.

15. Ibid.

16. Ibid.

17. Ibid., 132.

18. David Benner, *The Gift of Being Yourself* (Downers Grove: InterVarsity, 2004), 15.

19. Mary Jo Meadow, *Christian Insight Meditation: Following in the Footsteps of John of the Cross* (Boston: Wisdom Publications, 2007), 162.

20. Brian J. Pierce, *We Walk the Path Together: Learning from Thich Nhat Hanh and Meister Eckhart* (Maryknoll: Orbis, 2005), 8.

21. Thich Nhat Hahn, *Living Buddha, Living Christ* (New York: Riverhead, 1995), 9.

22. Ibid., 7.

23. David Entwistle, *Integrative Approaches to Psychology and Christianity* (Eugene, Ore.: Wipf & Stock, 2004), 230.

CHAPTER 2: THE GIFT OF CONTEMPLATION AND MINDFULNESS

1. Thomas Merton, *The Inner Experience: Notes on Contemplation* (New York: HarperSanFrancisco, 2003), 57.

2. Ibid., 58.

3. F.C. Happold, *Mysticism: A Study and an Anthology* (London: Penguin, 1973), 70.

4. James Finley, *The Awakening Call: Fostering Intimacy with God* (Notre Dame: Ave Maria, 1984), 21.

5. Mary Jo Meadow, *Christian Insight Meditation: Following in the Footsteps of John of the Cross* (Boston: Wisdom Publications, 2007), 129.

6. Finley, *The Awakening Call*, 22.

7. Meadow, *Christian Insight Meditation*, 163.

8. Ibid., 164.

9. Thomas Keating, *Open Mind, Open Heart: The Contemplative Dimension of the Gospel* (New York: Continuum, 2006), 4.

10. Ibid.

11. St. John of the Cross, *The Ascent of Mount Carmel* (Bibliolife, 2009), 117.

12. Augustine Baker, *Sancta Sophia, 1657.* See Robert S. Miola, ed., *Early Modern Catholicism: An Anthology of Primary Sources* (Oxford: Oxford University Press, 2007), 326.

13. *The Way of a Pilgrim*, trans. Gleb Pokrovsky (Woodstock, Vt.: Skylight Paths, 2001), 17.

14. Brian J. Pierce, *We Walk the Path Together: Learning from Thich Nhat Hanh and Meister Eckhart* (Maryknoll: Orbis, 2005), 97.

15. St. John of the Cross, *The Ascent of Mount Carmel and The Dark Night*, trans. John Venard (Darlington Carmel, 1981), 55.

16. Ibid., 54

17. Paul Tornier, *The Meaning of Persons* (London: SCM, 1957), 13.

18. Thich Nhat Hahn, *Going Home: Jesus and Buddha as Brothers* (New York: Riverhead Books, 1999), 84.

19. Jon Kabat-Zinn, *Full Catastrophe Living: Using the Wisdom of Your Body and Mind to Face Stress, Pain and Illness* (New York: Dell, 1990), 29–30.

20. Thich Nhat Hahn, *Going Home*, 124-25.

21. Kabat-Zinn, *Full Catastrophe Living*, 69–70.

22. Ibid.

23. Marsha Linehan, *Cognitive Behavioral Treatment of Borderline Personality Disorder* (New York: Guilford, 1993), 28.

24. M. Linehan, H. Heard, and H. Armstrong, "Naturalistic Follow-up of a Behavioral Treatment for Chronically Parasuicidal Borderline Patients," *Archives of General Psychiatry*, 50 (12), (1993), 971–74.

25. Zindel Segal, J. Mark Williams, and John Teasdale, *Mindfulness-Based Cognitive Therapy for Depression* (New York: Guilford, 2002), 65.

26. J. Teasdale, Z. Segal, J. Williams, V. Ridgeway, and M. Lau, "Prevention of Relapse/recurrence in Major Depression by Mindfulness-based Cognitive Therapy," *Journal of Consulting and Clinical Psychology*, 68, (2000), 615-23.

27. Daniel Siegel, *The Mindful Brain* (New York: W.W. Norton, 2007), 31.

28. Sharon Begley, "Scans of Monks' Brains Show Meditation Alters Structure and Functioning," *Science Journal*, (2004), B1.

29. Siegel, *The Mindful Brain,* 181.

30. B.A. Wallace, *The Four Immeasurables: Cultivating a Boundless Self* (Ithaca: Snow Lion, 2004), 11ff.

31. Meister Eckhart, Sermon Pr. 4, cited in Pierce, *We Walk the Path Together,* 17.

CHAPTER 3: CHRISTIAN CONTEMPLATION: A WAY OF LIFE

1. Rainer Maria Rilke, *Letters to a Young Poet,* trans. M. D. Heter (New York: W. W. Norton, 1993), 27.

2. Meister Eckhart, *Sermons and Treatises, Vol. 11*, trans. M. O. C. Walshe (London: Element, 1981), 1655.

3. Quoted in Brian J. Pierce, *We Walk the Path Together: Learning from Thich Nhat Hanh and Meister Eckhart* (Maryknoll: Orbis, 2005), 128.

4. Henri Nouwen, *Clowning in Rome: Reflections on Solitude, Celibacy, Prayer and Contemplation* (New York: Doubleday, 1979), 36.

5. From "Christus: A Mystery" by Henry Wadsworth Longfellow (1807 —1882).

6. Michael Cassey, *Strangers to the City* (Brewster, Mass.: Paraclete, 2005), xii.

7. Mark Epstein, *Going on Being: Buddhism and the Way of Change* (New York: Broadway, 2002), 30.

8. Martin Laird, *Into the Silent Land: A Guide to the Christian Practice of Contemplation* (Oxford: Oxford University Press, (2006), 27.

CHAPTER 4: CHRISTIAN CONTEMPLATION: A WAY OF BEING IN THERAPY

1. Douglas John Hall, *God and Human Suffering: An Exercise in the Theology of the Cross* (Minneapolis: Augsburg Publishing House, 1986), 56.

2. Ibid.

3. Kathleen Speeth, "On Psychotherapeutic Attention" *The Journal of Transpersonal Psychology* (14) 2, (1982), 153.

4. Ibid.

5. Paul Tornier, *The Meaning of Persons* (London: SCM, 1957), 160.

6. Speeth, "On Psychotherapeutic Attention," 151.

7. Christopher K. Germer, Ronald D. Siegel, and Paul R. Fulton, eds., *Mindfulness and Psychotherapy* (New York: Guilford, 2005), 68.

8. Ibid., 72

9. Tornier, *The Meaning of Persons*, 134.

10. Carl Rogers, *On Becoming a Person* (New York: Houghton Mifflin, 1961), 284.

11. Rollo May, *The Art of Counseling* (New York: Abingdon, 1967), 97.

12. Germer, et al, *Mindfulness and Psychotherapy*, 63.

13. Ibid.

14. Ibid.

15. Ibid., 78.

16. Ibid., 64.

17. Ibid., 65.

18. Theodor Reik, *Listening with the Third Ear: The Inner Experience of a Psychoanalyst* (New York: Farrar Straus Giroux 1983), 144.

19. Donald W. Winnicott, *The Maturational Processes and Facilitating Environment* (New York: International University Press, 1965), 60.

CHAPTER 5: CHRISTIAN CONTEMPLATION: A WAY OF ACTION

1. Brian J. Pierce, *We Walk the Path Together: Learning from Thich Nhat Hanh and Meister Eckhart* (Maryknoll: Orbis, 2005), 132–134.

2. Thomas Merton, *The Seven Storey Mountain* (Orlando: Harcourt Brace & Co, 1948), 3.

3. Thomas Merton, *The Secular Journal of Thomas Merton* (New York: Farrar, Strauss & Giroux, 1959), 8.

4. Ibid.

5. Thomas Merton, *Sign of Jonas* (New York: Harcourt, 1981), 323.

6. Henri Nouwen, *Encounters with Merton* (New York: Crossroad, 1972), 5.

7. Thomas Merton, *Contemplation in a World of Action* (New York: Image, 1973), 175.

8. Ibid., 172.

9. Jack Kornfield, *A Path with Heart* (New York: Bantam, 1993), 222.

10. Paul B. Pedersen, Juris G. Draguns, Walter J. Lonner, Joseph E. Trimble, eds., *Counseling Across Cultures*, 5th ed. (Thousand Oaks, Calif.: Sage Publications, 2002), 3.

11. Ibid., p.230.

12. Merton, *Contemplation in a World of Action*, 222.

13. Ibid.

14. Ibid.

15. Pierce, *We Walk the Path Together*, 135.

16. Derald Wing Sue, "Eliminating Cultural Oppression in Counseling: Toward a General Theory" *Journal of Counseling and Psychology* 25, 5 (1978), 419–28.

17. Larry Kent Graham, *Care of Persons, Care of Worlds* (Nashville: Abingdon, 1992), 43.

18. Merton, *Sign of Jonas*, 312.

19. Nouwen, *Encounters with Merton*, 86.

20. Quoted in Henri Nouwen, *Encounters with Merton*, 87.

21. Graham, *Care of Persons*, 17.

22. Ibid., 44.

CHAPTER 6: CHRISTIAN CONTEMPLATION: A WAY TO WORSHIP

1. See chapter 4 for a full description of CROSS.

2. James Finley, *The Awakening Call: Fostering Intimacy with God* (Notre Dame: Ave Maria, 1984), 76.

3. Ibid., 77.

4. Ibid., 41-42.

5. Ibid., 27.

6. Thomas Merton, *Contemplative Prayer* (New York: Herder and Herder, 1969), 33.

7. Ibid., 37.

8. Gerald May, *Will and Spirit* (San Francisco: Harper & Row, 1982), 5.

9. Henri Nouwen, *Behold the Beauty of the Lord: Praying with Icons* (Notre Dame: Ave Maria, 1987), 21.

10. Rowan Williams, *The Dwelling of the Light: Praying with Icons of Jesus* (Norwich: Canterbury, 2003), 57.

11. Anthony Kelly and Francis Moloney, *Experiencing God in the Gospel of John* (New York: Paulist, 2003), 346.

12. Ibid., 347.

13. Quoted in Fr. John Baggley, *Icons: Reading Sacred Images* (London: Catholic Truth Society, 2007), 11.

Bibliography

Anderson, Ray S. *Christians Who Counsel.* Grand Rapids: Zondervan, 1990.

Aten, Jamie D., and Mark M. Leach. *Spirituality and Therapeutic Process: A Comprehensive Resource from Intake to Termination.* Washington, D.C.: APA Books, 2008.

Augustine of Hippo. *St. Augustine Confessions.* Trans. Henry Chadwick. New York: Oxford University Press, 1998.

Baggley, Fr. John. *Icons: Reading Sacred Images.* London: Catholic Truth Society, 2007.

Begley, Sharon. "Scans of Monks' Brains Show Meditation Alters Structure and Functioning." *The Wall Street Journal: Science Journal,* November 5, 2004. http://psyphz.psych.wisc.edu/web/News/Meditation_Alters_Brain_WSJ_11-04.htm.

Benner, David. *The Gift of Being Yourself.* Downers Grove, Ill.: InterVarsity, 2004.

Butler, Cuthbert. *Western Mysticism.* New York: Harper & Row, 2003.

Cassey, Michael. *Strangers to the City.* Brewster, Mass.: Paraclete, 2005.

Clinton, Timothy, and George Ohlschlager. *Competent Christian Counseling.* Vol.1. Colorado Springs: Waterbrook, 2002.

Corey, Gerald. *Theory and Practice of Counseling and Psychotherapy.* Toronto: Thomson Brooks/Cole, 2008.

Delio, Ila. *Franciscan Prayer.* Cincinnati: St. Anthony Messenger, 2004.

Entwistle, David. *Integrative Approaches to Psychology and Christianity.* Eugene, Ore.: Wipf & Stock, 2004.

Epstein, Mark. *Going on Being: Buddhism and the Way of Change.* New York: Broadway, 2002.

Finley, James. *The Awakening Call: Fostering Intimacy with God.* Notre Dame: Ave Maria, 1984.

Germer, Christopher K., Ronald D. Siegel, and Paul R. Fulton. *Mindfulness and Psychotherapy.* New York: Guilford, 2005.

Goldberg, Carl. *On Being a Psychotherapist.* Lanham, Md.: Jason Aronson, 1997.

Graham, Larry Kent. *Care of Persons, Care of Worlds.* Nashville: Abingdon, 1992.

Hall, Douglas John. *God and Human Suffering: An Exercise in the Theology of the Cross.* Minneapolis: Augsburg Publishing House, 1986.

Happold, Frederick Crossfield. *Mysticism, A Study and an Anthology.* London: Penguin, 1973.

Hubble, Mark A, Barry L. Duncan, and Scott D. Miller. *The Heart and Soul of Change: What Works in Therapy.* Washington, D.C.: American Psychological Association, 2003.

John of the Cross. *The Ascent of Mount Carmel and The Dark Night.* Trans. John Venard. Darlington, UK: Darlington Carmel, 1981.

Kabat-Zinn, Jon. *Full Catastrophe Living: Using the Wisdom of your Body and Mind to Face Stress, Pain and Illness.* New York: Dell, 1990.

Keating, Thomas. *Open Mind, Open Heart: The Contemplative Dimension of the Gospel.* New York: Continuum, 2006.

Kelly, Anthony, and Francis Moloney. *Experiencing God in the Gospel of John.* New York: Paulist, 2003.

Kornfield, Jack. *A Path with Heart.* New York: Bantam, 1993.

Laird, Martin. *Into the Silent Land: A Guide to the Christian Practice of Contemplation.* Oxford: Oxford University Press, 2006.

Linehan, Marsha. *Cognitive Behavioral Treatment of Borderline Personality Disorder.* New York: Guilford,1993.

Linehan, Marsha, Heidi Heard, and Hubert Armstrong. (1993). "Naturalistic follow-up of a behavioral treatment for chronically parasuicidal borderline patients. *Archives of General Psychiatry*, 50 (12), 971–74.

Maloney, George. *Alone with the Alone.* Notre Dame: Ave Maria, 1982.

May, Gerald. *Will and Spirit.* New York: Harper & Row, 1982.

May, Rollo. *The Art of Counseling.* New York: Abingdon, 1967.

McMinn, Mark. *Psychology, Theology, and Spirituality in Christian Counseling* Carol Stream, Ill.: Tyndale, 1996.

Meadow, Mary Jo. *Christian Insight Meditation: Following in the Footsteps of John of the Cross.* Boston: Wisdom Publications, 2007.

Merton, Thomas. *The Inner Experience: Notes on Contemplation.* New York: HarperSanFrancisco, 2003.

———. *Contemplation in a World of Action.* New York: Image, 1973.

———. *Contemplative Prayer.* New York: Herder and Herder, 1969.

———. *The Secular Journal of Thomas Merton.* New York: Farrar, Strauss & Giroux, 1959.

———. *Sign of Jonas.* New York: Harcourt Brace, 1953.

———. *The Seven Storey Mountain.* Orlando: Harcourt Brace & Co., 1948.

Nouwen, Henri. *Behold the Beauty of the Lord: Praying with Icons.* Notre Dame: Ave Maria, 1987.

———. *Clowning in Rome:Reflection on Solitude, Celibacy, Prayer and Contemplation.* New York: Doubleday, 1979.

———. *Encounters with Merton.* New York: Crossroad, 1972.

Pedersen, Paul B., Juris G. Draguns, Walter J. Lonner, and Joseph E. Trimble, eds. *Counseling Across Cultures.* 5th ed. Thousand Oaks, Calif.: Sage Publications, 2002.

Pennington, M. Basil, Thomas Keating, and Clark Thomas. *Finding Grace at the Center: The Beginning of Centering Prayer.* 3rd ed. Woodstock, Vt.: SkyLight Paths, 2007.

Pierce, Brian J. *We Walk the Path Together: Learning from Thich Nhat Hanh and Meister Eckhart.* Maryknoll: Orbis, 2005.

Plante, Thomas. *Spiritual Practices in Psychotherapy: Thirteen Tools for Enhancing Psychological Health.* Washington, D.C.: APA Books, 2009.

Richards, P. Scott, and Allen E. Bergin. *A Spiritual Strategy for Counseling and Psychotherapy,* 2nd ed. Washington, D.C.: APA Books, 2005.

Reik, Theodor. *Listening with the Third Ear: The Inner Experience of a Psychoanalyst.* New York: Farrar Straus Giroux, 1983.

Rilke, Rainer Maria. *Poems 1906 to 1926.* Trans. Joan M. Burnham. Novato, Calif.: New World Library, 2000.

Rogers, Carl. *On Becoming a Person.* New York: Houghton Mifflin, 1961.

Rohr, Richard. *The Naked Now: Learning to See as the Mystics See.* New York: Crossroad, 2009.

Schlauch, Chris. *Faithful Companioning: How Pastoral Counseling Heals.* Minneapolis: Fortress Press, 1995.

Segal, Zindel, J. Mark Williams, and John Teasdale, *Mindfulness-Based Cognitive Therapy for Depression.* New York: Guilford, 2002.

Siegel, Daniel. *The Mindful Brain.* New York: W. W. Norton, 2007.

Skovholt, Thomas, and Michael Ronnestad. *The Evolving Professional Self: Stages and Themes in Therapist and Counselor Development.* New York: Wiley, 1992.

Speeth, Kathleen. "On Psychotherapeutic Attention." *The Journal of Transpersonal Psychology*, (14) 2, 153, 1982.

Sperry, Len, and Edward P. Schafranske. *Spiritually Oriented Psychotherapy.* Washington, D.C.: APA Books, 2004.

Sue, Derald Wing. "Eliminating Cultural Oppression in Counseling: Toward a General Theory." *Journal of Counseling and Psychology,* 25, no. 5, 419–28, 1978. (1978).

Teyber, Edward. *Interpersonal Process in Therapy, An Integrative Model.* 5th ed. Toronto: Thomson Brooks/Cole, 2005.

Thich Nhat Hanh. *Going Home: Jesus and Buddha as Brothers.* New York: Riverhead, 1999.

———. *Living Buddha, Living Christ.* New York: Riverhead, 1995.

Tornier, Paul. *The Meaning of Persons.* London: SCM, 1957.

Tracy, David. *The Analogical Imagination.* New York: Crossroad, 1992.

The Way of a Pilgrim. Translated by Reginald Michael French. New York: Harper Collins, 1965.

Wallace, B. Allan. *The Four Immeasurables: Cultivating a Boundless Self.* Ithaca, N.Y.: Snow Lion, 2004.

Williams, Rowan. *The Dwelling of the Light: Praying with Icons of Jesus.* Norwich, UK: Canterbury, 2003.

Winnicott, Donald W. *The Maturational Processes and Facilitating Environment.* New York: International University Press, 1965.

Vitz, Paul C., *Psychology as Religion: The Cult of Self-Worship.* 2nd ed. Grand Rapids: Eerdmans, 1977.

Index of Names and Subjects

Arasteh, A. Reza, 102
attention, 77–79

case conceptualization, 81–82
Cassey, Michael, 65
centering prayer, 36
Christian meditation, attentional
    and awareness, 36
Clinton, Timothy, 21
cognitive behavioral therapy, 16
compassion, 83–84, 96
    Rwanda, 106–9
contemplation, acquired, 34
    definition of, 8–9, 35
    infused, 34
    life of, 10–11
    mindfulness and, 9
    a way of being, 38
    a way of knowing, 35
contemplative counseling, as being
        with, 70
    CROSS, 85–87
    human condition and, 72–73
    human suffering and, 74
    process of change and, 75–76
contemplative: counselor, 11–12
    as icons, 117
    identity of, 23–25
    seeing, 61
    social action and, 99–101
counseling, Christian, 3
    contemplative, 9–10

dialectical behavioral therapy, 43

empathy, 83–84
Epstein, Mark, 26
equanimity, 84

Goldberg, Carl, 20

healing, holistic, 3
hospitality, 79–80
humanism, secular, 5–6

icons, 118
identity, formation of professional,
    18
    Christian counselor, 19–20
integration: types, 4–5

Jesus Prayer, 37–38, 116

Keating, Thomas, 36
Kornfel, Jack, 99

lectio divina, 113–14
listening, deep and genuine, 27
    as a spiritual habit, 116
loving-kindness meditation, 123

magnanimity, 26
    dialogue and, 27–28
McMinn, Mark, 21
Meadow, Mary Jo, 9
Merton, Thomas, 26, 96–99, 102,
    104–5
Mindfulness-Based Cognitive
    Therapy, 43

Mindfulness-Based Stress Reduction
    Program, 42
mindfulness, definition of, 40
    neuroscience and, 45
    psychotherapy and, 44
    religious character of, 49

Nouwen, Henri, 97

Ohlschlager, George, 21–22

prayer, 115
    and icons, 117
    for unity, 122

Rilke, Rainer Maria, 55

Siegel, Daniel, 44
solitude, 112–13
solution-focused therapy, 17
St. John of the Cross, 37, 39, 113
suffering, attitude towards, 33–34,
    42

The Holy Trinity, icon, 118–21
The Way of a Pilgrim, 37
Thich Nhat Hahn, 27, 41
Tornier, Paul, 78, 82

CPSIA information can be obtained at www.ICGtesting.com
Printed in the USA
BVOW022131180613

323653BV00006B/84/P